Serious Laughter

a guide book to a happier,
healthier, more productive life.

by Yvonne Francine Conte

Serious Laughter™
A guide book to a happier, healthier, more productive life.

by Yvonne Francine Conte

Published by:
> Amsterdam Berwick Publishing
> 262 Culver Road
> Rochester, NY 14607-2332

Printed and Bound by:
> Thomspn-Shore, Inc., Dexter, MI

Published in the United States of America
Second Edition
6 5 4 3 2 1

Conte, Yvonne. Serious Laughter: A guidebook to a happier, healthier, more productive life.

Non-fiction: Humor, Health, Family, Humor in The Workplace, Communication, Relationships

This book is intended for education and or entertainment purposes only. Readers suffering from depression or stress related illnesses should use their own judgment or consult a medical expert or their personal physicians for specific applications to their individual situations.

Illustrated by Anna Cerullo-Smith

For
Angela Torsella Conte
**may God bless you and
keep you laughing**

*"There are three things that are real
- God, human folly and laughter.
The first two are beyond comprehension.
So, we must do what we can with the third."*
- John F. Kennedy

Introduction

Some people think that you either have a sense of humor or you do not and that you can not teach someone to be funny. This book is not intended to give you a sense of humor or to turn you into a stand up comic. Most definitely, to try to make a person funny would prove to be futile. However I believe it is very possible to awaken the funny bone in people, if they want to add humor to their lives. You do not teach people to be funny, you merely give them permission.

Remember the Christmas story, A Christmas Carol, by Charles Dickens? Scrooge was a wretched, miserable, hardhearted, uncaring old sort. I would say he had no sense of humor at all in the beginning of the story. As the tale unfolds his attitude changes. The spirits of Christmas Past, Present and Future awaken the compassionate, charitable, thoughtful, happy heart that was there all the time, underneath all that selfishness and misery. Scrooge was able to find happiness only when he wanted it, by realizing it's value.

The same thing can be done with your sense of humor. If you really want to have more humor in your life, you can. We all have some element of pain or unmanageable times to go through in our lives. The mission of Serious Laughter, is to show the value of humor. Think of this book as a gradual awakening to the joys of laughter and an introduction to this wonderful vehicle that will help you through the difficult times and simply make the good times more meaningful.

Contents

Chapter One
The Thunderstorm Years

*"If you want the rainbow, you gotta put up
with the rain."* - Dolly Parton

It was 1990. I was 38 years old and fresh out
of my second divorce. With remarkable
endurance, I thought I had put the pieces of my
life back together quite nicely. For six perplexing
years we had hopelessly attempted to hold our
futile marriage together. He was an alcoholic.
When he was good he was very very good, but
when he was bad he was horrid. The six year
marriage depleted my energy, eliminated my
enthusiasm and left me with a much deflated self
esteem. Now that he was gone and that crisis
was behind me my life could be normal again. I
would get back to being me.

Like an exterminator ridding the house of it's
pests, I began to remove his memory. Every
stick of furniture, every picture, every tea towel

was sold or given away. With every
remembrance of him gone, I built a beautiful new
home and filled it with fresh new furnishings-
purposely choosing items I thought he would
not like. There! Not one trace of him. I was
safe, my children were safe. The same passion
that had loved him, was my obsession to put my
life flawlessly back together again!

With the mission completed, I could not
understand why I was so unhappy. Everything I
did seemed like a chore. Why was it so difficult
to get back to normal? What is normal anyway?

The following passage from my journal
illustrates just how defeated and despondent I
was.

July 10th, 1990
*"I have so much and I feel like I have
nothing. I just don't have the zip I used to have.
I know I'm strong but I feel weak. I know I'm
full of life but I just want to die. I know I'm
funny but I feel so very sad. Who am I really?
And why am I here? Would it matter if I
wasn't? And who would miss me? Or would
anyone? I have this wonderful family and I
can't stand to see any of them. I have this
beautiful house but it doesn't feel like a home.
I have a great job, making more money than I
ever have and I just want to quit. None of this
means anything to me. What in the world is
wrong with me? Everyone thinks I'm such a big
success, so why do I feel like such a failure?
How do you measure success? In material
things? In achievements? There must be
something wrong with me. I miss him and I*

loathe myself for that. I'm angry! And I have no one to go to with this anger. I have no where to take these tears."

Silently suffering with these feelings for just over a year, I was the cheerful neighbor, mother, daughter and friend that everyone expected me to be. Inside I was dying. Dreadfully lonely and sad, I kept my feelings locked up inside me until August 7th 1991. My life literally changed forever on that day.

On a dare, I stepped onto the stage at Wise Guys Comedy Room. It was a Wednesday night. Normally there were maybe ten customers on Open Mic Night. That is when 15 to 20 unknown comic wannabees step into the spotlight and try desperately and often times unsuccessfully to be funny.

All my friends, co-workers, customers and relatives were there. The room was bursting. Standing room only. They were all there to see me! This little principled, conscientious mother of two who didn't smoke or drink or do drugs. Who never said a foul word (in public). What in the world was I going to say that would be remotely interesting to these people? My good friend Lynda Carpenter gave me the best advice ever. She said, "Vonnie, just be yourself and tell them about all the ludicrous things you have been through, Your life is hysterical! Tell them about your ex-husband, your mother, your kids!" She was right. Sitting in the dark waiting for my turn, I did not realize how magical it would be. That night I began the best therapy money can not buy. Onstage I started to tell

everyone how I really felt. Every adverse
situation that happened in my life suddenly
turned into new funny bits for Wednesday Night
Open Mic. I could not wait to get there. This
was my opportunity to laugh at myself and at the
burdens that I had carried for what seemed an
eternity. It was such a pleasure to tell the world,
(or the ten people who showed up) that I was
embarrassed to be Italian when I was a child.
While our stuffy upper class WASP neighbors
had beautiful potted geraniums on their front
porches, we had tomato plants growing in rusty
coffee cans and braided garlic on the front door!
I began writing jokes about my father getting
old, my kids leaving the nest, my mother's
compulsion to make me eat and her obsession
to collect plastic bags, twist ties and margarine
tubs. Then I graduated to my first husband and
how I felt about men in general. All that anger I
had bottled up was finally beginning to spill out.
This felt extraordinary. I could say anything I
wanted on that stage. People laughed. The
crucial part was that no one was judging me. It
felt wonderful to come off that stage and have
someone say, "My husband was the same way
and it feels so good to be able to laugh about it."
Oh my God! There were other people in the
world who were going through the same anguish
that I was. This was magnificent news.

That laughter and acceptance was the
beginning of an amazing healing within my soul.
If you can laugh about what happens to you, you
can get through it. It felt so good to be on that
stage that it was the only place I wanted to be.

My friends and family did not understand me.

They must have thought I was completely out of control. I quit my job thinking that I would do stand up full time and become a big star! That was, predictably, the biggest joke of them all. What really happened was that very quickly, I couldn't pay my $1,500 a month mortgage payment and the bills began to pile up. I simply did not care. Now I could write jokes about being in debt!

To make this long story short...the bank finally took the house. I sold all my new furniture and moved to Rochester, N.Y. With the help of fellow comedian and friend, Mark Cooper, I got a job as an octopus on a children's television show which aired on the local Fox network. I continued to do stand up comedy on the weekends. My wonderful friend, John Gabriel and I shared an apartment and laughter for two years. We laughed about the strangest things, but we laughed really hard, at least twice a day.

One afternoon I received a call from a woman who wanted me to talk to her group for about twenty minutes. I assumed she was requesting a stand up comedy performance. During the course of the conversation I realized she was mistakenly under the impression that I was some sort of speaker or facilitator. She said they do not pay their speakers, however they would donate $50 to my favorite charity. She wanted me to talk for twenty minutes about the importance of humor in the workplace. What a great idea!

I never told her that I was not a speaker but

in fact a stand up comic. I ended up talking for
30 minutes in front of 100 members of The
National Society of Fund Raising Executives. I got
them to laugh. This room full of executive "suits"
- all laughing! It was the beginning of an
innovative and very rewarding career.

The very next day the director of a nursing
home in Galloway, Ohio called. Someone from
the meeting in Rochester had called and told
him about me. He wanted me to fly to Ohio to
speak at his managers meeting. I had no money.
I had no idea what to charge. I did not really
have an actual program put together. I took a
deep breath and in my best corporate voice said,
"Yes my fee is... and you would be responsible
for air fare and hotel accommodations." I closed
my eyes, crossed my fingers and held my breath
and the voice on the phone said, "Great! I will
have my assistant take care of all the details." I
got off the phone, ran into John's room and he
and I danced the "I can not believe it" dance. We
were ecstatic! I went to the library and began to
read everything I could get my hands on about
humor.

One of the most interesting pieces of
information I acquired was that there is more
information in the library about humus than
there is about humor. I find humus: the dark
organic part of the soil formed from decaying
matter, to be pretty boring and could not imagine
why anyone would write twenty-six books about
it. On the other hand, I find humor to be
fascinating. I decided right then and there that
my next project would be to write a book about
humor and how it can be used to produce better

lives for all of us.

Serious Laughter is the product of many hours of research, typing, observing, talking with others and listening. It has been a wonderful learning experience for me. I hope reading this book will prove to be interesting, educational and entertaining for those who read it.

I have discovered something to do in my life that genuinely has meaning. I pray a lot and I trust my Higher Power. For the past few years I have been asking Him for direction. I am so grateful for the answer to my prayer.

"Pain nourishes courage. You can't be brave if you've only had wonderful things happen to you."
- Mary Tyler Moore

Six Steps to Reach Your Mountain Top

Have a mission statement

Write a mission statement to which you are passionately committed. Write long term goals and short term goals that will be the steps you take up your mountian.

Have something at risk

Understand why you are striving for your goal. What do you stand to loose if you quit the climb?

Be a problem solver

Always look for creative solutions. Never blame or complain. Find your way around the boulder.

Visualize your success

How will you feel? What will you be wearing? What you will you say? Who will be there when you reach your mountain top?

Seek feedback

Ask for feedback from mentors and colleagues. Be able to look at your work objectively. "Am I on the right trail?"

Have balance in your life

Remember that to a truly successful person, church and family always come first. Find time for them in each day. A workaholic is not a successful person. Without balance you may fall down the mountain.

Who you are, is God's gift to you.
What you do with who you are, is your gift to God

Chapter Two
Stress and Worry

"The way I see it, if the kids are still alive when my husband gets home from work, then I've done my job." - Roseanne Barr

A recent Gallup Poll found that 40% of Americans feel stressed out everyday and 39% are stressed out some of the time. It is a fact that 80% of all visits to the doctor are for stress related illnesses. Stress is also the number one reason for workman's compensation claims.

Whether you sell babushkas or Buicks, raise farm animals or children, perform brain surgery or stand up comedy, stress is out to get you.

We all know what it is like. We work from eight to five and then rush to pick up the children from daycare. We take Johnny to soccer practice and Susie to swim lessons and have dinner on the table by six. Phones keep ringing, mail keeps coming! Deadlines loom, restrictions stand in our way, due dates approach! Cars break down, babies cry, kids slam doors, cats pee on the rug and dryers eat socks every single day! We all face the danger of going crazy or at least getting angry, hurt, offended, appalled, perplexed, aggravated, frustrated and yes, stressed out. It is my belief that stress is not an event, it is our reaction based on our perception of an event. We are free to alter our perceptions. *Praise God!*

There is a better way to handle the craziness. We all know that exercise, meditation, proper nutrition, sufficient rest and visualization are good ways to reduce our level of stress. But do you know that humor and laughter are by far the most effective techniques we have available to us for coping with stress? In order to fix the problems we face we have to define them. Let us begin by taking note of all our stressors.

In order to get the full value of everything we will read in this book we have to be open! We have to be sure we are not going to think about what we have to do later today or tomorrow or about that family member who needs us to do something for them.

Right now take out a sheet of paper and make a list of all the challenges you are currently facing.

This list should have all the worries, concerns, projects and tasks that need your attention. This is a sample of what your list might look like.

✓ I need to fill the car with gas.

✓ I'm coming down with a cold.

✓ I have to be at the meeting early tomorrow.

✓ I hate my hair today.
✓ I am worried about my mother's health.
✓ I am behind on several bills.
✓ My son hangs around with the wrong kids.
✓ The mortgage is due again.
✓ I miss my father. I can't believe he is gone.
✓ I hate being single.
✓ I have to pay my car insurance today.
✓ I have to remember to pick up milk.
✓ Susie needs new sneakers.

On this list should be very serious concerns as well as the silly ones about which we all worry. It should include anything and everything that causes us stress. Now take the list and crumple it up and toss it in the waste basket or, if you really are into it, take it into the living room, place it in the fireplace and watch it burn. This really is very therapeutic. I promise you, I will show you a better way to handle these concerns. They will not just go away, in fact they may even get worse while you are reading this book. The point is that you cannot do anything about any of that right this minute so just relax and concentrate on the ideas that lie before you. My hope is that the ideas we share will help you to plan a better way to handle your worries and concerns.

Now, is there anyone out there who could not think of anything to write down on their list of concerns? I hope not. That is the first sign of insanity! We all have situations in our life that could cause us to worry and complain. That's not going to change. What we can change is the way we see things; our perception and the way we handle our problems; our actions.

Some researchers believe that 75% of all conversation today is negative. You know that is true. The first thing people comment on in the morning is the weather. It is never good enough! They always have to complain. "It's so hot out today!" They can not stop there either. They have to make sure you understand just how miserable they are. They want you to feel their pain. "It's so hot out there that I stuck to the seat of the car. My chocolate bar melted and got all over the seat and now I have to get that mess cleaned up. I should have just stayed home today!"

Negativity is everywhere. It had been rainy and cold for several days in Syracuse, New York but this morning was glorious. The sun was brilliant. The air was warm and you just couldn't have asked for a better day. Especially in Syracuse, where sunshine makes headlines! In the hotel lobby I stood watching as people began to walk into the conference room. A man about fifty years old was getting out of his car. He had his crumpled raincoat over his arm. He reminded me of the television character, Columbo. When he came in I said with enthusiasm, "Good Morning. Isn't it a beautiful day?" He said with disgust, "Yeah, in this town you never know what to wear!"

Some people are just never happy unless they are unhappy! With that thought I would like to introduce you to one of my favorite relatives, Aunt Frances. She is a small woman, about 4'11" with a very petite frame. I do not want to say she is negative, but when she smells flowers, she looks around for a coffin. Aunt Frances never ceases to have some story or event to tell me. To her they are serious, but to me they are usually hysterically funny! Like the time she told me she was shrinking and was worried that one day she would wake up and be so small no one would be able to find her!

Aunt Frances was always complaining about something. Nothing was good or right or happy. She was so ridiculous about her complaints that it was really funny to listen to her. She could find fault with found money! And she did!

She also loved to go to funerals and even went to those of people she did not know. I think she liked the attention. I was with her once when she went to calling hours for a friend. We went into the funeral home and she sat up front with the family and wept with the best of them. Then on the way out she looked into another room and saw another wake going on. She took my hand and looked up at me. Her eyes lit up and with her mischievous smile, she winked and said, "Come on let's go!" Before I could say no we were crying in that room too. I have no idea who it was who died but we mourned for him anyway. I remember that Aunt Francis told the grieving widow, "He looks so good. I can't believe he's gone!"

Famous Aunt Francis complaints were, "I can't eat nothing with these damn teeth the doctor gave me!" or "Yvonne, I'm telling you my grandson, (granddaughter, daughter, neighbor or whomever...) is going to drive me crazy!" Aunt Francis used to start every conversation with, "You don't know what I go through..." or "You don't know what they done to me!" And I always thought...you're right, I don't know and I don't want to know, but I'll bet money, you're going to tell me!

Do not tell other people your problems. Eighty percent do not care and the other twenty percent are kind of glad it happened to you. The truth is we all have troubles. Every single human being on this earth has troubles. Some days you're the bug, some days the windshield. Rich or poor, tall or short, black, white, green or yellow, everyone has troubles. Complaining about them does nothing but upset you and everyone within hearing distance. Worrying only lessens your ability to constructively solve the problem. Worrying adds stress to the list of difficulties you need to handle and inhibits your ability to concentrate.

I always say, "What benefit do I stand to gain?" If there is no benefit, then why waste the effort? Even though there is no constructive benefit to complaining or worrying, we continue to worry about the strangest things. Do you worry about getting struck by lightning? Your chances are only one in 350,000. Ever worry about being buried alive? Only a one in 10 million chance for that one!

Some people get all stressed about something as simple as the weather while others handle serious situations like death or serious illness, with the grace and courage of a Jackie Kennedy. What is the difference? Why do we need to know the difference? Because the higher the stress level in a person or company the lower the productivity.

Let's look at ways that may put us in a better mood so that we can do something constructive about the troubles, concerns and difficulties we all face - all those things on our list.

There are only two ways to solve a problem. Either you change it or you accept it the way it is. A nationally known time management company believes the number one characteristic of successful people is the ability to separate the vital situations from the trivial ones. The best way to do that is to ask yourself, will this really matter to me five years from now? If the answer is no, then it is trivial! Think of some situation that you are currently facing that has you worried, concerned or stressed out. Answer these questions before you start to worry or complain. Do I have anything to gain by worrying? Who would like to hear me complain? O.K. now that we know there is no benefit to complaining and worrying, what can we do to better handle our concerns?

The Dale Carnegie Institute teaches a simple yet effective way to handle worry and stress. "First, analyze your situation. Next, ask yourself, what is the worst that can happen? Prepare to accept the worst that can happen, if necessary. Once you have accepted the worst that could possibly happen, calmly proceed to improve on the worst." It sounds too good to be true, doesn't it? If you stop to think about it, this is just plain common sense. This is the advice we would give to our dearest friends who were in the middle of a stressful or worrisome situation. The problem is that when we are in the middle of troubled water, we do not use common sense. We act based on emotion. That is where we get into trouble. Try to look at your problems as if they were someone else's. Carnegie suggests that we ask ourselves three questions:

1. What am I worrying about?
2. What can I do about it?
3. When can I begin to take action?

It makes sense that if you actually say, "What am I worrying about?" You give yourself a chance to step outside of your situation and really look at the hard cold facts. This eliminates any misunderstanding or confusion and helps you to stay focused on the actual problem or concern. Once you can look at a situation objectively, you are better equipped to see several solutions. Once you have a few options, you are in a better place to develop a plan of action. The only way to change or improve a situation is to do something about it!

EXERCISE #1

Develop An Action Strategy

This exercise will work much better if you really brainstorm for the answers and write down all of them...even the absurd ones. Do not be afraid to throw some humor into the mix. Try to be as open and creative with your answers as possible. Do not judge! Just let that resourceful mind of yours work for you. To illustrate how this works I'm going to use a situation some of us face.

Step #1.

State your concern in one/two concise sentences. This is how things are. The facts:

I cannot seem to find the time or energy to get enough exercise.

Step #2.

Complete this thought. If I had a magic wand I would wave it and this is how I would want this situation to be.

I would have a specific uninterrupted time each day for exercise and I would never miss a day for any reason, ever!

Step #3.

List five things I can do to make a positive difference right now.

1. Take a Calgon bath and de-stress myself while I work on a plan
2. Read a motivational book to get me going
3. Make a list of the benefits of exercise
4. List people I know who regularly exercise and look and feel great
5. Invest in a good control top pantyhose

Step #4.

List five things I can do to make a positive difference in this situation in the future?

1. Set aside a specific time of the day to exercise
2. Exercise with a buddy
3. Develop a plan of action to use when I do not feel like exercising
4. Make a positive affirmation tape to listen to every morning
5. Reward myself for good exercise behavior with a trip to the movies

Step #5.

List any resources skills, knowledge, people or organizations that may help me.

1. Enroll in an aerobic or dance class; join a gym
2. Get involved in a sport of some sort
3. Read Make The Connection by Bob Greene and Oprah Winfrey
4. Spend time with my friends who like to exercise
5. Make an appointment with my doctor for a check up and advice

Step #6.

What are possible obstacles.

1. *Lack of time*
2. *Lack of Enthusiasm*
3. *Excuses and Interruptions*
4. *Boredom*
5. *Fear of Failure*

Step #7.

Acceptance. If I cannot make a difference, what can I do to accept this situation?

This one I have control over. I can make a difference. I don't have to accept it.

O.K. now you take a situation in your life and try this exercise to make your life a bit easier! Good Luck!

Step #1.

State your concern in one concise sentence. This is how things are.

_____

_____

Step #2.

Complete this thought. If I had a magic wand I would wave it and this is how I would want this situation to be.

_____

_____

_____

Step #3.

List five things I can do to make a positive difference in this situation right now.

_____

_____
_____
_____
_____

Step #4.

List five things I can do to make a positive difference in this situation in the future?

_____
_____
_____
_____
_____

Step #5.

List any resources skills knowledge people or organizations that may help me.

_____
_____

Step #6.

What are possible obstacles.

_____
_____

Step #7.

Acceptance. If I cannot make a difference, what can I do to accept this situation?

_____
_____
_____

Now Laugh! Yes laugh and here's why...
Dr. Norman Cousins, in his best selling book, _Anatomy of an Illness as Perceived by the_

Patient (Bantam, 1983), takes an interesting look at the use of humor to overcome a painful and debilitating illness that even heavy medications were unable to relieve. Dr. Cousins found that ten minutes of good belly laughter gave him two hours of pain-free sleep. I find that to be amazing information. Laughter is a pain reliever. (Move over Tylenol!) His doctors said he was going to die so he called on his own personal strengths and healed himself from within with the help of laughter. He began to watch humorous movies and read funny books.

Cousins also said, "I've never known a person, who possessed the gift of hearty laughter to be burdened by constipation." Just another benefit of laughter I thought I would make a note of just in case anyone is suffering.

He believes, like I do, that illness itself is not a laughing matter. He says, "Perhaps it should be. Laughter is a form of internal jogging. It moves your internal organs around. It enhances respiration. It is an igniter of great expectations."

It is absolutely true! If it has been a while since you have had a good chuckle, you are missing out on one of your body's best antidotes for stress and anxiety. A good hearty belly laugh stretches the muscles from the diaphragm all the way to the scalp. That stretch releases the tension that causes fatigue stress and headaches. A good laugh will also exercise the muscles in your tummy. I am told that twenty seconds of belly laughter is equal to three minutes of strenuous rowing. I am not a great lover of exercise so every morning I stand buck naked in front of a full length mirror and I laugh and laugh. The older I get the easier it is to laugh! Come on all you fuddy duddys who never crack a smile. I dare you to go right now to the nearest mirror, strip naked and start to sing that 70's tune, *Feelings*. Trust me, you will laugh.

However, if you are at work, the naked part might be a problem. Try this instead. Sit back in your chair and grab hold of your belly. (If you do not have one just hold on to a co-worker's belly. Be sure to ask permission first.)   Now laugh as hard as you can. Can you feel how the muscles in your tummy are working when you laugh? What a great way to tighten those flabby tummy's! You can almost feel a boost in circulation and oxygen in the blood. That can give you a giant burst of energy. Some researchers suggest laughing may even release endorphins, the body's natural painkillers and mood lifters. Isn't this great? And it is absolutely free. You do not need any special equipment or clothing, you do not have to belong to a fancy club and do not have to shower afterward! It was Milton Berle who said, "Laughter is the best medicine in the world." Laughter is the same in any language too. Think about it!

The next time you are stuck in traffic and the waiting is just driving you out of your mind, try reacting differently and see if your results change. Remember that getting all tense and irritated won't speed up the traffic any. Calm yourself down by taking a few deep breaths. Try singing to a tune on the radio. Distract yourself by doing some people watching. Look in the mirror and smile at yourself. Flirt with yourself.

Laugh at yourself! Stick out your tongue.

The truth is you feel better when you laugh and smile. So why wouldn't you want to do what makes you feel better? Maybe you are a bit skeptical. O.K. I will prove it to you. Try this right now. Look into a mirror and growl at yourself. I mean I want you to look your absolute worst! Look at your self like you are the nastiest, most hateful person ever! A total grump! Now take a deep breath and look into that mirror again. This time smile the widest smile you can. Lets see those pearly whites! Now, do you notice any difference in the way your body feels when you smiled compared to when you growled? You feel different. You feel better. You have just experienced the power of your smile. Why not fake it till you make it? I promise you, you will not make any friends going around looking like the picture on your drivers license. So try a smile. Come on , it will not kill you.

Smile even when things are not the best that they can be. At least now you know you will feel better. If you feel better, then just maybe, you will be in a better frame of mind. If you are in a better frame of mind, then just maybe, you will be able to handle that problem or situation you're facing in a more productive way. If you want to be happy, act happy.

Make that load you're carrying a little bit lighter each day by adding laughter and humor to your life, one smile at a time. Be wacky, go crazy, be a fool! It is so good for you and everyone around you. Remember you can make an absolute fool of yourself. I promise it won't kill you or make you appear stupid and you may even make new friends - people love to be around fun individuals!

I want to express to you how important laughter is physically. This description of the clinical effects of laughter is something I believe everyone needs to know.

When you laugh, the neural passages inside your brain commence to reverberate. Electrical and chemical impulses begin running expeditiously throughout your body as if in a race for the gold. The pituitary gland is aroused; hormones and endorphins wake up your bloodstream by flashing through your blood like an alarm. The serum cortisol decreases, furnishing an antidote for the unhealthy effects of stress and worry. Your body temperature rises half a degree, your pulse rate and blood pressure decrease, your arteries and thoracic muscles withdraw, your vocal chords tremble, and your face twists and turns. Your abdominal muscles get conditioned and exercised. Pressure grows in your lungs. Your ventilation benefits by helping reduce a prolonged respiratory environment. An enzyme secretes that shields the stomach from forming ulcers. Endorphins that provide natural pain relief are released. Instantaneously your lower jaw becomes unmanageable, and your mouth opens wide. Breath explodes from your mouth at nearly 70 miles an hour. Oxygen and nutrients move easier to the body tissues. I am not sure, however, I think this is good for you!

This chapter deals with a problem that is so very easy and yet seems to be the most difficult for us to remedy. How to deal with stress and worry! Sometimes the answer is right in front of us, but we just can not see it. Sometimes it is right under our nose. We all have a choice to live our lives as we see fit. That is where the answer lies, in the choices we make.

I received the remedy years ago without realizing it. In 1976 my life was filled with stress. I had so little money that most of my clothing came from a thrift store. This hand written note on a crumpled slip of paper, was found in the pocket of a jacket I purchased at The Nearly New Shop, in Chattanooga, Tennessee. It was $2.97 well spent. I kept the note because I thought it was a "nice little saying". Years later I realized it's value.

"Have faith in God
Sleep Well
Love Good Music
See the Funny Side of Life
...and health and happiness will be yours"

Time Management

Stress happens when we are just plain overloaded! Why do we always think we have to handle every little detail? Do yourself a favor and let someone else take control. Use this memo and you will be helping others to grow, while you help yourself to a managed life.

Have this little memo ready and waiting the next time you get an unwanted interruption:

Crisis n. turning point, climax, emergency, critical stage.

Please do not interrupt me unless it is a **crisis**:
Ask yourself these four questions prior to coming to me for help:
1. What is the challenge?
2. What are the possible solutions?
3. Which do <u>you</u> recommend?
4. Do you still need to see me?

Also please note: **Remember the Don't cry over spilt milk rule:**
If you can think of a way to improve a situation, by all means let me know so we can improve it. Do not, however, whine and complain about how bad things are unless you have an idea to share on how to make it better!

EXERCISE #2

Woe is Me Log

This is the beginning of your stress reduction plan. First we have to identify the things that typically cause us stress. Then we will find a way to overcome them using the creative powers of humor. Let's get started.

Create an ongoing list of the stress in your life. Be specific. Write down exactly what causes you to worry, loose your temper, overreact or become irritable. Make 21 copies of the Woe is Me Log. Keep track of the events, people or situations that cause you stress for 21 days.

Example:

Situations   traffic jams

Quirks   people who are not dependable

Habits   people who sniff instead of getting a
              tissue

Things   dust

Events   family holiday dinners

People   specific...Mary - constantly talks
              about nothing
              general...stupid people

My Woe is Me Log

Situations

_____
_____
_____

Quirks

_____
_____
_____

Habits

_____
_____
_____

Things

_____
_____
_____

Events

_____
_____
_____

People

_____
_____
_____

Anything we didn't cover?

_____
_____
_____

The Perfect Gift

(I found the next two poems on the bathroom wall at a Wallmart Store)
Authors unknown

A SMILE costs nothing
but it creates so much.
It enriches those who receive it
without impoverishing those who give it.
It happens in a flash and the
memory of it sometimes lasts forever.
A SMILE creates happiness in the home,
fosters goodwill in a business
and is the countersign of friends.
It is rest to the weary, daylight to the discouraged,
sunshine to the soul
and nature's best antidote for trouble.
It can not be bought, begged, borrowed, or stolen,
for it is something that is of no earthly value,
until it is given away.
And, if it ever happens that some people
should be too tired to give you a SMILE,
Why not leave one of yours?
For nobody needs a SMILE
as much as those who have none left to give.

The Scare of the Week

Our air is polluted, the water is too,
fish that swim in it are not good for you,
fruit and fresh veggies, luscious you say?
Don't eat them ever with pesticide spray.
Salt is bad, sugar is worse,
beer and cigarettes, for sure they're a curse.
Avoid dairy products, say no to red meat.
Our cholesterol levels must go in retreat.
Coffee and decaf which you thought was O.K.,
may boost your cholesterol day after day.
Get rays off the sun, your skin will just fry,
stay in the house and with radon you'll die.
Don't walk in the woods, you can really get sick.
Lime disease comes from a pin head size tick!
If one thing wont get you, another one will.
Don't worry, be happy, because worry can kill!

37

Chapter Three
Pain is Inevitable
Suffering is Optional

"I'm in pain...I should produce a show at Radio City: Night of One Hundred Anxieties...My mother bought a Jewish satellite dish, it picks up problems from other people's families...For the holidays I bought her a Menorah on a dimmer and a self complaining oven..." - Richard Lewis

What does the Positive Power of Humor mean? It is the Power of Humor that positively affects both our mental and physical health. It is the Power of Humor that positively affects our ability to cope with crisis and change effectively. Whether it is life or a horse that throws you, it is the positive power of humor that gets you right back on. One of America's favorite TV Dad's, Bill Cosby, said, "You can turn painful situations around through laughter. If you can find the humor in anything, you can survive it."

Humor is a set of developed skills. I believe that we are not born with or without a sense of humor, but that it is just simply how we choose to look at the world. And it really is a choice. "Through humor, we see in what seems rational, the irrational; in what seems important, the unimportant." - Charles Chaplin

The root word in Latin for Humor is umor: to be like water. To be fluid or flexible is a great way to think of your sense of humor - that it is your ability to be fluid or flexible, especially in the face of crisis or change.

Laughter, to begin with, is an intensely personal experience. What is funny to one person may not be funny to another person. In many ways what makes you laugh is as private as what makes you cry. We are the only creatures on the face of the earth with the ability to laugh. I think there must be a reason that we were given the gift of laughter. Maybe it is so we can all cope with mother-in-laws and ex-spouses, who knows? Recently, I agreed to drop off my son John at a halfway point so he could be a part of his father's family reunion. I called my former sister-in-law to get directions. As luck would have it my ex-husband answered the phone. After 20 years of being my "ex" you would think he could handle giving me directions over the phone. Instead he called to his sister to do the chore, "Marie, it's the plaintiff!" I am still referred to as the plaintiff? You have to learn to laugh at this kind of behavior or you can drive yourself crazy. Is that any way to address the

mother of his children? No. Was it funny? Yes,
I believe it was. I justify it this way: if that were
a scene on last night's situation comedy, I would
have laughed. Almost everything that happens to
us would be funny if it happened to someone
else. We have to learn to see the absurdities in
our everyday life and laugh them off. It really is
a choice. Do I want to get stressed out over this
or do I want to find the humor in it and laugh it
off?

A lot of how we react to what happens in our
day has to do with how we feel about ourselves.
And how we feel about ourselves has everything
to do with how we perceive a situation to be.
Our perception of the situation, how we really
see it, determines how we react to it. If we can
change our perception, we can change our
reaction and in the end change the results.

Remember, Pain is Inevitable, Suffering is
Optional. You have to choose not to suffer.

Please do not misunderstand me here.
There are times in our lives that cause us real
pain. To some extent we have to go through the
experience of suffering in order to heal. I have
been there. When I say suffering is optional, I
am talking about those of us who choose to
continue to suffer by constantly complaining
and doing nothing to make the situation better.
We choose to suffer when we only see the
darkness and never the end of the tunnel.
When we say negative destructive things like, "I
can't" or "I wont", "It will never change" or "I
could never do it" or "It never works out for
me" When we think like this we are absolutely

right because there is no way we can move on to a better place if we constantly think about how much we suffer. A good way to see if you are one of the Proverbial Suffering Complainers is to ask yourself the Yes-But question. When someone offers you a way out of your misery do you answer with a "yes-but"? Is there always a reason why you can not accomplish things? Do you catch yourself saying, "Yes - But", "I could have - but...", "I wanted to...but...", "I tried to...but..." Joni Mitchell said "it all comes down to you" I believe there is no try - you either do it or you don't! Your willingness creates your ability. When you do not take any action to change a situation, please understand, that is your choice. You have just chosen to stay in your misery. You have chosen to continue to suffer.

Let's take a look at how we got all stressed out in the first place. How do we get from happy go lucky children to nervous frightened adults?

Research from the book of American Averages tells us that children laugh on an average of 400 times a day! By the time we reach adulthood we reduce our laughter to only 15 times a day! If laughter and humor is so important to our mental and physical health, then we had better find out how we got from a hearty 400 to only 15 laughs per day. We had better find out how we can get back to laughing our way to good health. By the time a child is only three years old he or she has heard "NO" 350 thousand times! "No!" "Put that down!" "Don't touch that!" "Stop it!" "No! No! No!" All this negativity...no wonder we stop laughing.

Think about when your children were babies or being around babies in general. What is the first thing we all attempt to do when we pick up a tiny baby? If you said, "make the baby laugh or smile" you are among the majority. We all make goofy faces and weird noises to try to get the baby to laugh or smile and then when the little one does we praise. "Good baby!" The baby grows to be a cute little toddler and again we reinforce that laughter is good and right. When our toddlers do anything remotely funny we laugh and once again let it be known that we appreciate that wonderful sense of humor...until this child gets to be about eight or nine years old. Then when he or she starts to act silly we say, "What's so funny young man?" "Wipe that silly smile off your face little girl!" "You better straighten up and act like a lady." "Grow up." "You'll never be successful unless you get serious." "No one respects a wise guy!" "Quit acting so silly!!!" We are teaching our young people that in order to be successful, in order to gain the respect of our peer group, we had better be dead serious! I don't know about you, but I don't want to be anything that starts with DEAD!

We really need to look at and reassess the messages we are sending our children about laughter and humor. Our children's sense of humor will either blossom as he or she grows older or it will begin to wither away. Please don't let it wither away! They then become that horribly stiff person in the office who just can't have fun. This is the person who , to be politically correct, is "Humor Impaired". He is too busy being important to laugh. He is the guy or gal who always has to rule the roost. The problem is by ruling the roost all the time we get so stressed out, all we end up doing is laying big fat eggs that everyone else in the roost has to clean up.

The serious people in our lives are often seen as distant, negative, arrogant or intimidating. Do you want others to read that from your face as you walk the office hallways? Is that what you want the people to think of you when you push your cart down the isle at the store? If you are not distant, negative, arrogant or intimidating, then quit looking so serious! There was a time in my life when people would ask, "What's wrong?" and I would answer, "Nothing, Why?" The response would always be the same, "You look mad." I wasn't mad yet I looked angry all the time. I was just preoccupied with worry and my face told the story. I think it is important to inform your face that you are happy. Even while you have situations to take care of that may not be the most fun to have to handle. Try to play the part of a happy person on the outside and it will make a difference as to how you feel on the inside. Angels fly because they take themselves lightly! If you want to fly, lighten up!

It used to be a fact that the one person in the office who found the funny in any given situation was perceived to be the "dingbat" or "The Corporate Airhead". That perception is changing now that we understand how much more a person can accomplish in a fun and relaxed atmosphere. To find out if you have a humor deficiency, take this Humor Deficiency Quiz.

1. How many times a day do I laugh out loud?
a. Never. It's not polite
b. Once/twice out of nervousness
c. Constantly, people are always asking me what is so funny?

2. Do I joke about my own shortcomings?
a. What shortcomings?
b. Why draw attention to myself?
c. Yes it's the best way to overcome them

3. How many of my friends are really funny?
a. I have no friends, only associates
b. One, but he embarrasses me
c. Most of my friends are stand up comic wannabees

4. When was the last time I did something silly, just for the fun of it?
a. Third grade but I don't like to talk about it
b. Last Halloween
c. Yesterday at the grocery store I held a banana to my nose and did my best Jimmy Durante impression

5. How many times a week do I find humor in; - a bumper sticker? - a greeting card? - a cartoon? - a TV commercial that wasn't meant to be funny? -something really stupid I saw some one else do?
a. I only read the Wall Street Journal
b. I read bumper stickers in order to keep my mind off my driving
c. I laugh constantly at everything I see! Life's a riot!

6. What % of the movies I see are comedies?
a. I only watch corporate training videos
b. 10% - I relate to Woody Allen movies
c. I only see comedies! I love to laugh and eat
   popcorn at the same time

7. When was the last time I told a joke?
a. Third grade but I don't like to talk about it
b. I try but I can never remember the punch
   line! I get embarrassed.
c. I'm the center of attention at parties with
   all my jokes!

Scoring your quiz: Add up how many a. b. &
c. answers you had. If you answered mostly a.
answers you are severely humor deprived and
need a transfusion. Go to the nearest video store
and rent National Lampoons Christmas Vacation
and My Cousin Vinny and force yourself to laugh!
Your life depends on it.

If you had mostly b. answers, you have
potential but need to relax more. Stop worrying
about what other people think of you because the
truth is...nobody is thinking of you!

If you are a c. person congratulations! Go
forth and make this world a funnier place! You
are Humor Healthy!

Unfortunately, our offices and boardrooms
are still filled to capacity with serious people!
They suffer from "ATP", Acute Terminal
Professionalism! They are so uptight, so
stressed out, so overworked that it's hard for
them to find the time to think, much less
accomplish anything! It's not because they have
no sense of humor. It is because they have been

conditioned to think they have to be dead serious to be respected and to be successful. THAT IS JUST NOT THE CASE!!! SO RELAX!!

Here are some great ways to reduce the stress level in your office or workplace. They are easy and for the most part cost nothing but a few minutes of your time and a bit of effort and creative thinking.

Appoint someone the CFO Chief Fun Officer each week. This person is responsible for bringing cartoons to put up on the bulletin board or on the back of the bathroom stall doors or next to the elevators. Give that person a fancy title. Everyone loves a title. Humorologist, Vice President in charge of Humor, The Humor Coordinator or how about The Fun Therapist! He or she must also bring a funny story or joke, (P.C. of course) to start off the Monday morning meeting. Start a humor suggestion box. Anyone who has a good idea for having more fun at work may drop the idea in the box. Make a game of it by picking the best idea each week and offering a silly prize. Socialize with fun uplifting people both at work and in your personal life. You will always attract positive or negative, people and circumstances that are in harmony with your dominant thoughts. If you think funny and constantly feed your mind with fun thoughts you will attract people who are also fun. Start a photo album to keep in the break room and fill it with funny pictures of co-workers. Better yet baby pictures of co-workers. Some offices encourage people to bring in their high school yearbooks. Reading what people wrote in yearbooks is almost as funny as looking at the ridiculous hair styles. Your imagination is the highest kite you can fly, so really let it soar.

Keep a scrap book of the funniest cartoons you can find. Look in magazines and newspapers for ones that relate to your particular job or someone at work. Keep it in the lunch room and encourage everyone to add to it.

Your boss isn't crazy about you having fun at work! What is he? Crazy? Having a happy team will only get you to the finish line sooner. Don't be afraid to suggest humor therapy to your boss. Be the leader. Remember, the lead sled dog is the only one with the decent view.

Let's think about how humor is used to promote business. How many television commercials do you recall off of the top of your head? How many of the ones you recall are funny or have some element of humor connected to it?

"Where's The Beef?" "I've Fallen And I Can't Get Up!" "Bud, Wise. Er." "Got Milk?" Yes, this billion dollar advertising industry realizes the power of humor!

Did you know that 10 of the first 15 radio programs were comedy programs? Right now there are over 35 shows in which comedy is a major ingredient on regular networks prime time TV schedules. Billboards, television, radio, magazines, newspapers, t-shirts, coffee mugs, pens, pencils, drink bottles, and on and on and on use comedy, fun and humor to get the message across. How many of your favorite shows are comedy related? How many of the top rated movies are comedy? Even the serious movies usually have a few good laughs in them. Why? Because people love to laugh! What a revelation!!! Who knew?

It makes sense to me that if you are in a better mood you will be more productive. It pays to have a happy crew! More and more companies are realizing that humor in the workplace is very definitely a positive force.

Recently syndicated columnist, Pat Buchanan had this to say about the effect Sonny Bono had on our Congress. "The late Congressman Bono humanized the United States Congress with his quick wit, fine sense of humor and warm genuine smile." In our United States Congress, Humor is being recognized as the tool of the new millennium.

Besides, it's a medical fact that the loss of fun and joy in your life is the first sign of mental illness. Reintroduce yourself to your sense of humor. Be silly once in a while. Reconnect with the child in you. Find your joy. Your health depends on it. Start at home. Tuck a lottery ticket into your significant others brief case, pocket or lunch. Take your granny to lunch for no reason. Buy flowers for a stranger. Mow your neighbors lawn. Walk down a busy street and put quarters in parking meters that are about to expire. Fold someone else's laundry. It really is wonderful to do these things. It will put you in such a great mood. Take fun seriously. You can stop the world's worst day dead in it's tracks by doing something just for the pure joy of it.

Remember, you can be as happy as you

decide to be. If your life isn't what you think it should be, try to see it from a funny perspective. "I call my doctor up. Told him I had diarrhea. He put me on hold! Story of my life...no respect." - Rodney Dangerfield

EXERCISE #3

 Learn to Laugh at Yourself

Describe three incidents that involved you doing something or saying something that embarrassed you. Choose something that while it was happening, you were not able to laugh at. Make a note of how long it actually took before you could laugh about it.

1. _____

_____

2. _____

_____

3. _____

_____

Think of a time when you or someone you know used humor to ease a tense situation?

_____
_____
_____
_____
_____
_____
_____

EXERCISE #4

How Did You Get So Serious?

We are all born with a wonderful sense of humor. As children we laugh and play without a care in the world. We laugh at everything... until someone tells us not to!

Exercise: Who was your humor suppressor?

Who said: Act like a lady! Grow up! Stop acting so silly! Be a man!

Begin to search back to your earliest memory and identify your humor suppressor. What was said to you or in your presence that could have suppressed your sense of humor? Who said it?

1. _____
2. _____
3. _____

What kinds of adult humor suppressors have you heard on the job?

1. _____
2. _____
3. _____

In your home? Church? Neighborhood?

1. _____
2. _____
3. _____

"Laughter need not be cut out of anything since it improves everything!" - James Thurber

Seven Steps to Humor Filled Life

1. Keep really funny people in your life
   -make friends with the funniest person at work
   -stay connected to the funny friends you have

2. Buy silly things that keep a smile on your face
   -keep toys at the office
   -always have a sponge clown nose on hand

3. Start a humor library
   -read funny books written by, for or about
   comedians
   -collect funny cartoons
   -collect tapes/videos/books that make you laugh

4. Watch humorous movies/TV shows
   -rent Three Stooges/Marx Brothers videos

5. Attend fun filled events
   -plan a monthly humor night with co-workers
   -start a humor night with neighbors/friends

6. Attend fun filled events
   -hire a stand up comic for your next work function
   -post up new cartoons each week
   -create a humor break room
   -learn to laugh with others and at yourself

7. Make other people happy
   -hire a clown to visit a sick friend
   -send a humor first aid kit to someone in need
   -dress up in a funny costume and surprise
   someone
   -smile goal: "Today I'm going to give away 20
   smiles!"
   -do something for someone and expect
   nothing in return

Chapter Four
Life Without Laughter

"Life is wonderful. Without it you're dead."
- Red Skelton

If you do not learn to use your humor tools to reduce the stress and worry in your life, the results can be fatal!   According to many doctors, stress and worry can cause the following: insomnia, types of paralysis, nervous stomach, ulcers, premature aging, wrinkles, loss of concentration, heart disease, headaches, nervous breakdowns, high blood pressure, hair loss, fear, and weakness of the immune system. O.K. maybe this is not fatal, but with all this going wrong a person can not possibly get anything done!

How can you be productive if you're all stressed out? My daughter Aubry asked me for a Coach Bag for her birthday. Anyone have a Coach bag? A small one can cost as much as

$200.! I didn't get stressed out about it. I went to K-Mart got her an "assistant coach bag". Five bucks! You just can't lose your mind over silly things like that. Choose to laugh! Make a joke. It works!

When I got my divorce back in the 70's I had no job, no education, no experience. I had gone to finishing school. I knew how to finish! What I did have were two little preschool children who looked up at me with those wide innocent eyes for everything. What's a mother to do? I was in Chattanooga Tennessee, nine hundred miles away from home. I was alone and frightened. I did what any young mother would do in this situation. I went to the mall.

I went to every store in the mall and applied for a job. Since I had no work experience most shop keepers just said, "Sorry, Sugar, nothing for you right now". Then I walked into a Merle Norman Cosmetics store and Miss Betty hired me! She looked at me up and down and then said in her aristocratic southern drawl, "What ever possessed you to apply for a job in my store?" I told her I applied in all the stores and wasn't going home without a job. She liked my attitude. From six in the morning until two in the afternoon I made cheese and meat trays for the Swiss Colony Cheese Store, then from five to nine at night I worked for Miss Betty at Merle Norman Cosmetics. On Saturdays I swept hair at a hair salon and every night I made homemade breads and sweet rolls that I sold on consignment at a local country club. I was exhausted. But I wasn't on welfare. I wasn't behind on any bills and my kids were fed and clothed! I considered this to be a tremendous success!

After six months of being a success I could barely walk without assistance. My hands and feet were full of pain and I couldn't figure out what was wrong with me. I looked old and I felt old! I guessed that since my father suffered with rheumatoid arthritis that must have been what was wrong with me. I took aspirin and just kept going until one day I noticed my hair was falling out. Now I could live life in pain, but no way was I going to live life bald! I went directly to the doctor. He said that I did have arthritis and that my level of stress was just aggravating it. He also said that if I didn't get a hold of my <u>stress</u> I would be in a wheel chair before my fortieth birthday. Stress was killing me.

That's when I began to study stress and learned how to get it under control. I found that the best way to control stress is with a good sense of humor. The more I studied it the more I was convinced that laughter and joy and happiness were my keys to a stress free life and a way for me to keep my hair.

Just knowing that doesn't solve anything. I had to make some changes in the way I conducted my life. I had to learn to relax. But how? I had to support my children. DILEMMA! I sat down with my good friend Carolyn Hale who simply asked me what I enjoyed doing. We made a list of all the things that I really enjoy doing; activities that I enjoyed at work or with my children or my friends; things I like to do alone or with groups of people. From that list we found out that at that time in my life among other things, I enjoyed the outdoors, playing in the dirt with the kids, hiking, tree climbing, getting dirty, taking things apart and putting them back together again. Carolyn then asked me how much money I needed to live. Then she sat back in her chair and said, "Well from the looks of things you would make a good construction worker!" We both laughed. I was 5'2" tall, weighed 105 pounds and was selling perfume and cheek color at a make up store! Not your average construction worker type. After we stopped laughing I told her I probably would be a good flag lady! We opened up the phone book and got in touch with the "Women In Construction" program.

After a few interviews I was accepted into the program. I quit all my jobs and began ten months of paid training in all phases of construction. I then applied to the Carpenters Local Union for a position as an apprentice carpenter. I got the job. Working forty hours a week gave me enough money to support my children and the time to enjoy them. Eventually I was able to save enough money to return to upstate New York to be near my family.

To reduce the level of stress in your life, first identify what is causing the stress. I was completely overworked. Why? Because I had four part time minimum wage jobs. I never saw my children. I was so overworked I had no energy to enjoy anything.

Find a way to rid your life of stress. Make changes in your life. Find a better paying job or move to a different area. Ask for help. Accept help. Educate yourself. Do what ever you need to do to rid your life of stress. There is only so much a person can handle. If your life is killing you, make some changes. Remember, it's all about the choices we make.

The ten months in the training class and the six years I spent as a union carpenter were not without situations that could have been stressful. I chose to laugh! When the man at the local union in Chattanooga said, "I may have to hire you but I don't have to keep you." I asked him point blank why he didn't like me. He said, "You ain't never gonna make it. You got four strikes against you little girl: You're a woman. You're too short. You're Eye-talian (Italian). And you're a Damn Yankee" In the end I found that he was right in only one of the four instances. I was too short.

Laughter and humor really helped me to overcome some of the situations I found myself in. I remember once on top of a ten story building in the center of town the journeyman to whom I was assigned said to me. "Now you be careful up here and if you do fall off the building tuck your head down between your knees." I asked naively, "Will that break my fall?" He said. "No but you'll be in a good position to kiss your sweet butt goodbye cause you are gonna die if you fall off this building!" Each day brought a new practical joke or prank. These men tortured me. They dipped my new Levi Jean jacket in sheet rock mud and hung it up to dry. When I went to put it on to go home, I found it hard as a rock. When I put my tool belt down to go take a break they fastened it to

the concrete floor with a high powered Hilti gun
that used 22 caliber bullet pins. My lunch box
was a constant area of fun for them. They took
all my food out and nailed the lunch box to the
floor then put all the food back in. When I
reached down to get my lunch, I fell flat on my
face. This was really funny to the guys. I was
continually sent on wild goose chases to find
tools that didn't exist. Two handled crowbars
and left handed hammers don't really exist.
Who knew?

Once when I went into the outhouse that sat
up on the top floor someone nailed it shut and
then hooked it to the crane and took it off the
building with me in it. Never mind that if it fell
I could have been killed! When I got out of the
outhouse I was covered with the worst kind of
stench you can imagine. I knew they were all up
there laughing at my expense. I also knew they
wanted me to cry and to quit. It just made me
stronger. I decided to play it their way. The
next day I brought in two delicious chocolate
sheet cakes. I told the guys on the crew that if
they left me alone all week with no practical
jokes I would bake them a surprise every
Friday. They were delighted and proceeded to
eat the cake. The next day the majority of them
were out sick. Must have been the chocolate Ex-
lax! Now who's laughing!?? They left me alone
after that episode.

Someone once said that life is 10% how you
take it and 90% how you make it. That is so
true. In any situation you have the right to
choose. Why not choose to see things in a
lighter way?

In order to do that you have to be looking for the lighter way. Look for the fun. Hear the laughter. Let me show you what I mean.
Quickly read out loud what you see.

Jack and Jill went

went up the

the hill to fetch a

a pail of wine.

If you read, "Jack and Jill went up the hill to fetch a pail of wine", you were incorrect. Look back and read it again. Did you notice that the words, _went_, _the_ and _a_, are printed twice? The fact is we only see what we expect to see. You expected that Jack and Jill went up the hill, so that's what you read. That's what you saw. Even though that's clearly not what was there.

If you're not looking for the funny side then chances are you will not find it. Be on the lookout for the funny things that happen in your day. Expect funny things to happen. Expect to have fun at work or in the grocery store. Expect to laugh at the dentist office. Expect to stumble over humorous things and you will see them and hear them and sometimes even smell them.

Our power to create through expectation is amazing. Here is a story with three lessons. Life is really funny. Our minds are really powerful. Perception is everything.

Donnarae is my older sister, my best friend and my hero. She was diagnosed with diabetes when she was five years old. Her life has been a mixture of visits to the hospital, pokes from the needles and adjusting her sugar level to keep from going into shock. It is a miracle to me how she always finds something to laugh about. Several years ago she lost her eyesight. With the help of numerous operations she is able to see out of one eye, just barely. One day she went down the cellar to let her dog Toby out. She came upon a "pile" of dark droppings. "Toby!" she yelled, "I can't believe you did this in the house. You know better than that!" she scolded. She put the dog out and because she couldn't see well enough to clean it up, covered the pile with newspaper and went upstairs. She was bothered all day by the smell of the pile Toby had left in the cellar. I happened to phone her that day and remember her saying that her whole house stunk! She said she couldn't even eat lunch it was so bad. Donna couldn't wait for her husband Gene to come home and clean it up. She said it was making her sick. Finally Gene arrived. He went down to clean up the mess Toby had left. He lifted the newspaper to find a chewed up black rubber hose! Donna's perception of what that pile consisted of had caused her to imagine that her whole house smelled like dog doo! We only see, hear, and, yes, even smell, what we expect to!

EXERCISE #5

Great Expectations

What do you expect for yourself? Dream big. Dream without boundaries. Go for the gold. Write down what you think your every dream come true would be. What is your ideal environment? If nothing were standing in your way, what would you be doing? In what career would your best self emerge? Where do you want to live? What are your expectations? Once you have great expectations, they will become your destiny!!

_____

_____

_____

_____

_____

_____

Chapter Five
Laugh? I'm Too Busy Crying

"My grandfather was a very insignificant man, actually. At his funeral, his hearse followed the other cars." - Woody Allen

When we lose someone we love it is always a difficult time. We go through so many feelings; shock, denial, anger, sadness, blame, loneliness, abandonment. It also seems to be a time when our sense of humor can be one of the best tools we have to really get us through those tough times.

The people I meet always have funny funeral stories for me. Here are some that were told to me by participants of the Humor Workshop.

The Socks
by Carla Jonquil

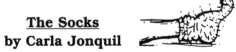

On the way to the cemetery I solemnly sat in the back seat of the car with my Mother. Ahead

of us, the black limousine carried my
Grandfather's coffin. I was crying, so my Mom
reached into her purse to get a tissue. "Oh no!"
She looked up startled. "What's wrong, Mom?" I
asked as I looked at my mother's hand holding a
pair of brown socks. "Dear God", she said
quietly, "I was supposed to give these socks to
the funeral director for Grampa. I hope they put
some socks on him."

We have been laughing out loud about the
socks for decades and are still wondering if
Grampa is up in heaven now barefoot!.

Let Go Please!

A pretty young girl told this story about how
she and two friends thought it would be fun to
crash the calling hours of a stranger. (Some
people have a strange sense of humor - but, hey,
that's O.K.)

She and her two friends went up to the
casket and knelt down as if to pray. Just then
her earring fell into the casket. She nervously
reached in to get it and the chain on her watch
caught on the deceased's button. She pulled her
hand out of the casket but couldn't get the watch
chain off the button. She panicked and began to
cry. Just then the priest came up and patted her
on the back and said, "He's in a better place now
child." She said, "I know but he's trying to take
me with him!"

I'm not dead yet!

Everyone waited patiently for their names to
be called to get into the funeral procession.
Some of the men stood at the back of the room

talking quietly. The names were called and people began to solemnly file out and get into the waiting cars. All of a sudden the name Gladys Magnella was called. From the back of the room an old hard of hearing uncle said loud enough for all to hear, "Oh my God I thought she died!" Mrs. Magnella turned to her daughter and said, "I told you, you don't take me out enough!"

Give credit where credit is due!

I took my father to the funeral of a friend of his. I noticed that my father was the best dressed and most well groomed gentleman in the room. After we got home I was telling my mother about it. I said, "Mom I'm so proud of Dad. He always looks and smells so good. The other men were wearing old, smelly, stained suits and the all looked like they needed haircuts and shaves. I wonder why they all look so unkempt?" My mother looked at me and said, "Their wives are all dead."

Heavy Weight
by Betty Ann Smith

Our family got a chuckle recently at the funeral of Bud, our dear friend who had lived with us for years as part of our family. My husband Rex walked beside the casket with the other pall bearers. As they got ready to lift the casket from the car to the church, someone said, "I hope this isn't going to be too heavy." Rex smiled and lovingly said, "It wont be too heavy. It's light. It's Bud-Light!"

Standing on Solid Ground

My husband and I attended the funeral of our neighbor Mrs. Able, who must have been in her late eighties. As we stood at the grave sight my husband nudged me and said, "Look. It's Mrs. Able's mother and father!" I looked up shocked and scanned the crowd looking for people who must be over one hundred years old. "Where?" I asked. My husband chuckled and then pointed to the next grave and whispered, "You are standing on them."

If you find yourself stealing funeral flowers you just might be a red neck...
by Sheila Creasman

She was my Dad's *loving devoted sister* who hadn't spoken a civil word to him in over ten years! There she was running around the funeral home all broken and sad about her eldest brother's car accident and untimely death. Yet, while the rest of the family went to the cemetery immediately following the funeral, she stayed behind stealing flower arrangements, along with the most expensive and largest gifts to take home for her and her younger sister.

In the end we did get back everything that was stolen. After the anger died down I began to laugh about the situation, thinking to myself - "If you stay behind at the funeral home to steal flowers while the rest of the family goes to the cemetery...you just might be a red neck!" Jeff Foxworthy could get enough material from my family alone to write an entirely new two hour HBO Special and never have to repeat a single story.

After retrieving the items from my aunt you would think that she would behave herself. No! The famous aunt struck again. She told some people that my step mother "had" my Dad killed for the insurance money. I was livid at first and my stepmom was talking about suing her for slander. After we talked about it I told my stepmom we could play my aunt's game. If she continued to gossip unjustly, I promised to call her and tell her that it's true. My step mother really arranged the whole thing! Unfortunately, since she figured it all out and was talking about it to everyone, we are going to have to shut her up. Remember we have connections and she's next on the list. Not for insurance mind you, but as a favor to my poor uncle who hides in his barn just to stay away from her!

The Most Fun at a Funeral Award
by Marilyn P.

I've left a list of my favorite jokes for my family to tell at my funeral. There is one in particular that I love to tell but that no one ever seems to understand! I want that one told at my funeral and no one gets to leave until they get it!

Deadly Mistaken Identity
by Don Cicchino

It was our first time ever inside a funeral home. My best friend and I sat in the last row. We didn't really want to be there, but we felt we should attend. A teacher from our school had passed away after suffering from a long battle with cancer. She was only 32 years old. We had never seen a dead person before. Her beautiful dark auburn hair had turned a dingy gray and her face was wrinkled and thin. I commented to my friend how bad she looked. We were two hot shot tough guys from the Italian neighborhood, however, in that room on that day, we were close to tears and almost afraid to look at what was before us.

A man sat beside us and asked how we knew the deceased. We told him that she used to be our teacher. He looked confused then asked us who we had come to see. It turns out that we were in the wrong room. We were at the funeral of an 86 year old woman who had simply died of old age.

"I don't mind death.
I just don't want to be there when it happens."
- Woody Allen

I know what it is to wonder if you will ever laugh again. On September 27th, 1995 my dear sweet Daddy went to heaven. Before he left us he spent four pain filled months suffering in the Veterans Hospital in Syracuse, New York. He was 85 years old.

He fell and broke his hip one night and had to be operated on. We all sat in the waiting room - aunts, uncles, cousins, sisters, children and grandchildren. Someone brought cannolis for the nurses. (Italian people always bring pastries where ever we go!) The doctors had given Daddy only a 25% chance of survival because his heart was so weak. We sat waiting and praying and drinking bad coffee out of flimsy paper cups. I

couldn't find anything to laugh about. The fact
that my Dad was in pain and there was nothing I
could do about it, was very frustrating to me. I
looked at the frightened look on my mother's
face and I knew there was no way I could help
her. I was afraid for her. Just then someone
turned to my sister and said, "After we leave here
take me to the mall. I want to get a new black
suit." I couldn't believe it. Immediately I began
to think of the lessons daddy had taught us.
Daddy always said, "Plan your work and work
your plan" and I remember him telling us to
"picture it - plan it - produce it!" But he also
said, "a winner never quits and a quitter never
wins"! Were we giving up too soon? Or were we
just planning ahead? Some call it being
realistic. I was so upset. I wanted to stand up
on a chair and say, "Hey, how about some
positive thoughts here? How about we begin
figuring out how we are going to take care of him
after the operation, not on what we will wear at
the funeral!" It seemed that everyone just
expected him to die that night. Everyone except
me. I just couldn't imagine my life without him.
He made me laugh. He made us all laugh. He
was the light that helped us all to see our
futures. I couldn't imagine that light going out.
Not yet. I wasn't ready. I went out into the hall.
I cried and I talked to him. I know that he
couldn't really hear me, but somehow I know he
got the message. I told him we were not ready to
let him go yet. I told him that if he left us now,
Mom would fall apart and my sisters would all
be basket cases and quite frankly, I wasn't ready
to face that. I couldn't face that. I wasn't strong

enough. I needed some time to adjust to the thought of not having my father's guidance to help me through.

I don't remember just how long it was. I know it seemed like an eternity. The doctor finally came out and said with a smile, "He's a trooper!" I knew it! I knew he wouldn't let me down! We all hugged each other and cried and hugged some more. (Italian people cry and hug when ever the moods strikes them. Happy or sad it really doesn't matter, we cry, we hug, we eat!) We filed in to see Daddy in the intensive care unit. His leg and hip were tied up to this metal thing and tubes were coming in and going out of his body from various spots. He looked weak and frail. As everyone gathered around his bed looking at him as if he had died, I decided it was time to find the funny. I leaned down close to my father and said in my best Mafia voice, "I only have one question for you Pop. Where did you hide the money?" The nurse began to laugh and Daddy even tried to smile until Mom rolled her eyes at me and said, "Everything's a joke with you."

Everything's not a joke with me. I just thought we could all use a laugh to break the tension we were all under. I just wanted to give my father a laugh. And I'm glad I did.

For the next four months my sisters and my mother were able to give Daddy the love and care that he needed. They were there every day. Day and night. They were there to wipe his face and comb his hair. They kept him clean and comfortable. They adjusted his tubes and rubbed his sores. They fed him and kissed him

and sat by his bed and cried for him. They
talked to the doctors about his medicine, his
breathing, his heartbeat, his blood pressure, his
stool and urine and blood count and how much
mucus was in his lungs. It drove me crazy some
of the stuff they would talk about. I can't deal
with that. It's making me sick right now just to
write about it. I don't know why. I just am no
good with illness and hospitals. I get sick to my
stomach when I step into a hospital and smell
that fragrant hospital mixture of disinfectant,
rubber gloves and dead flowers. I always feel
like germs are crawling all over me when I'm at a
hospital.

My sisters and my mother, on the other hand,
should have all been nurses because they seem
to come alive in that atmosphere. They will
happily wipe up, probe into, mop up, poke at,
pick at or inspect anything that oozes, drips, or
leaks without batting an eyelash. I remember as
a kid someone was always standing there with
her head tilted back, mouth wide open, tongue
out and someone else was starring down it with a
flash light as if looking for Jimmy Hoffa or
something. I gag, choke and eventually pass out.

I remember that I felt useless the entire time
Dad was in the hospital. I wanted to do
something to help him, but to be honest about it,
I hated being there. I was afraid that Dad would
think I didn't love him if I wasn't there hovering
over him in that hospital room every day and
every night like everyone else.

I had to do what I knew how to do. It had to
come from my heart. So I did what I could to
bring cheer into Daddy's hospital room. I put up

pictures of comedians and jokes on the wall at the foot of his bed.

We all knew he would never come home. I wasn't going to let his last days with us be so full of sadness and despair. I told him funny stories every time I came to visit. I always had some way to make him laugh or smile whenever I saw him. I came in with a clown nose on or a goofy hat. Anything at all to humor him. I usually got the nurses to laugh and sometimes even the doctors. I know in my heart that Daddy loved it. That's all that mattered.

I thought about how I treated my Dad while he was alive and that helped me. He knew how much I loved him and Mom.

My Dad and I laughed a lot together. I loved to take him places because we always managed to get into trouble. He could find something funny in any situation. That is what I loved most about my Dad. He really knew how to have fun. I imagine that's why he lived such a long and happy life.

I took him to the drug store once. I always drove up to the door and helped him out of the car, walked him in and got him a cart. Then I would go back out to park the car. This time when I went back into the store to find him, I noticed a nice Halloween display with one of the ugliest masks I had ever seen. I quickly put the mask on and went to find Dad. There he was slowly coming around the aisle with the cart. I pounced out in front of him and said, "Stick 'em up!" He proceeded to pretend that he was having a heart attack right there in the store in front of everyone. Two men immediately grabbed me and held my hands behind my back. They asked Daddy if he was O.K. He continued to act as if he were terrified of me. He really should have received an Oscar for his performance. I stood there with the ridiculous mask still covering my face. I tried to tell the men that he was my father and we were just playing, but no one took me too seriously. One gentleman asked Daddy reluctantly, "Is this your daughter?" With a confused look Daddy said, "I don't know who she is!" I told Dad that he better tell them what was going on or I would be headed to the police department and he would be walking home. Needless to say we were not allowed in that store anymore and they made me buy the mask. I used the mask that year to decorate the Thanksgiving turkey. I still have it and I laugh every time I see it.

We all love in our own way. Mine is to always find the funny in life and to share that with the ones I love. Sitting at the hospital wasn't easy for me. I had to force myself to do it and I had to bring something funny with me to get through it. So that's what I did.

Mom, my three sisters, their husbands and I all went to the funeral home to pick out the casket the morning after dad died. It was so strange to be with this group of typically funny people and find absolutely nothing to smile or laugh about. It was like I were sitting there with strangers. I remember how absurd I thought everything was. The funeral director actually brought my fathers suit coat in to try to match it to the lining of the casket. How strange.

In order to appreciate this next story you

have to know a bit of background about my
father. He sold stainless steel cookware for
thirty years. Selling pots and pans was a big
part of his life. To say that he was good at it
would be a gross understatement. He loved to
sell and his customers loved him. Our family
room is filled with huge trophies and plaques to
commemorate his life in stainless steel and his
exceptional sales ability.

On this day, in that room, looking at all the
different coffins, I felt like I was at a used car lot.
This one was solid mahogany. This one had
brass handles. This one was made of oak. This
one would last a lifetime. What??? Then this
emotionless man pointed to the ugliest casket in
the room and said, "This one is solid stainless
steel". My mother said, "He was in stainless
steel all his life. He should be in stainless steel
for eternity". We all cracked up. That was so
funny to us. My mother would like me to clarify
that we did not really bury him in a stainless
steel casket. We settled on a beautiful bronze one
with all the apostles having The Last Supper
along the bottom. I thought that was so
appropriate for dad. The thought of dad going to
heaven at a big long table full of food was perfect
since he loved to eat. I just hope the apostles
cooked The Last Supper in stainless steel pots.

Even in the darkest hour, you can find
something to be thankful for. I was so thankful
that we had not lost our ability to laugh. You
can, if you really try, look for something that will
break the tension, reduce the stress, and get you
through the really tough times.

After spending over ten thousand dollars at the funeral home, we drove out of the parking lot toward the cemetery to pick out the plot. My mother noticed that my sister Donna's car door was ajar and said to the limousine driver, "Hey, stop, my daughters door is open." I said, "Gee we're not even out of the parking lot, already they're trying to drum up new business!" Once more we were able to laugh.

Every one of us experiences some amount of burdens in our lifetime. Choose not to allow them to paralyze your progress.

"Humor is another of the soul's weapons in the fight for self preservation. It is well known that humor, more than anything else in the human makeup, can afford an aloofness and an ability to rise above any situation, even if only for a few seconds."

- Victor Frankl, <u>Man's Search for Meaning</u>

Chapter Six
Finding Your Funny Bone

"Words with "K" in it are funny.
'Cupcake' is funny... 'Tomato is not funny.
Cleveland is funny. 'Maryland is not funny..."
- Neil Simon, "The Sunshine Boys"

If we can change our mood we can change our future. To live in the past is to drive into the future looking in the rear view mirror. You can not control the wind, but you surely can control how you set your sail.

This is all helpful advice. However, how do we take control of the situation with humor? How can we turn a difficult task into an easy one? What do we do to turn anger into a smile? This next story will illustrate how a young man in England turned an otherwise annoying situation into a great funny story.

There is nothing funny about getting a speeding ticket! Or is there? The following article appears courtesy of the Rochester Sunday Democrat and Chronicle.

Just The Ticket

"A speeding British motorist caught by a roadside camera tried to play a little joke when police sent him a speeding ticket. The notice included a photograph of the car, the date and the speed and demanded payment of a £65.00 fine.

The motorist sent back a picture of a check, according to the police superintendent Deryck Farmer, in Crewe, in North West England.

Police sent back a photograph of a pair of handcuffs! The motorist got the message and mailed the real check."

This incident undoubtedly brought laughter to a great many people who might otherwise have been stressed out or angered by it. The fact that it was in the Sunday paper in Rochester tells me it must have appeared in countless other papers bringing laughter to readers all over the world and now to the readers of this book.

Getting a speeding ticket is never fun! You have to go out of your way to make it fun. One time a police officer decided to punish me by making me wait in my car almost fifteen minutes before he even came to get my license. Realizing what he was up to, I decided to use the time wisely. Taking out some files and my computer I began to get some work done while I waited. I had things to do, people to see, places to go. I was more upset that he was making me wait so

long than I was about getting the ticket. I was in
a hurry after all - that is why I was speeding in
the first place! When he came to the window I
acted as if I were engrossed in my work that I
hardly noticed him. I just didn't want to give
him the satisfaction of thinking he upset me. I
smiled and said hello and offered my license. He
said, "Do you know how fast you were going?" I
said, "No, not really. I admit I wasn't paying too
much attention." He said, "Oh, so if I told you
that you were going 90 m.p.h. you would just
have to take my word for it?" I laughed and told
him I didn't think my car could go that fast.
Angry, he said, "You think this is funny? This is
serious!" I took a deep breath and in the kindest
voice, told the biggest lie I ever told, "I'm sorry
young man, but I only have six months to live, so
to me nothing is too serious!" I took the ticket
and thanked him for it. He was nearly
speechless and began to apologize and tell me
how dreadful he felt. I told him not to even give
it another thought and drove off smiling. I loved
it. I made him feel ghastly for giving me that
ticket! The funny part of the story happened
when I told my mom about it.

She said, "You should never have lied to that
police officer, Yvonne. What if he stops you six
months from now? Then what are you going to
tell him?" I answered, "I'll just say, please don't
give me a ticket officer, I just lost my twin sister
and I'm just not myself today!"

The result was that I still got a speeding ticket,
still had to pay for it and still got marks on my
license. By finding a way to see humor in this
situation, I was able to relieve myself of the stress

related to receiving traffic tickets. I got something else too. This great story came from that incident. I've been telling my friends and laughing with them about the twin sister story for a few years now. Almost every time I tell the story it prompts someone else to tell a good speeding ticket or traffic story. The laughter never ends.

When you are in the middle of something upsetting, take a moment to think of anything at all that could be funny about it. Tell yourself that you are really going to laugh more about the things that happen to you; the things that happen to all of us. Start with what you feel comfortable with, then work on more to laugh about. Refine your humor. You will find that you will become more charismatic as time goes on. Adding humor to your life will only enhance everything else that is already you!

For those of you who still think you either have a sense of humor or you don't, I offer you this logic. Let us just say that you want to learn how to paint a beautiful picture. You tried but you just were not very good at it. Everything you painted looked disastrous to you. You decided that no matter how much you would like to be a good painter you realize you are just not talented and so you give up. You just failed as a painter.

What if you stuck with it? What would happen if you decided to enroll in an art class? Do you think it would be helpful if you got some books out of the library and began to study the artists that interested you? If you started to spend time with other artists and went to galleries and museums and made a goal to paint every day, how would that effect that way you painted? I think soon you would see a difference in your ability. You can learn to paint and you can learn to relax and add more fun to your life too. You just have to want to and you have to take action. Even if you are the meanest old goat, there is still hope for you as long as you want humor in your life and take action. That is the key.

When my daughter Aubry was five years old she told me she wanted to be a singer. Ordinarily this would not have alarmed the average mother. I cringed. My daughter was a terrible singer. I used to call her *One Note Lucy.* When Aubry sang at the top of her lungs, the dog left the room, the paint on the wall pealed and some of my plants died. My only hope was that as she grew older her yearning to be a singer would fade. It just got stronger. She pleaded passionately for singing lessons. I offered her anything and everything else. She took tap, ballet and jazz lessons for several years and then quit. Bass guitar lessons lasted only three weeks. I enrolled her in a modeling class. After the first fashion show she quit. Then I bought her a trumpet which became a decoration in her room after just five lessons. I tried to interest her in anything but voice. The kid just could not hold a tune! When she was fifteen she befriended a young girl who just happened to be the best singer in her school. She just happened to take voice lessons. Aubry went with her friend, sat on the couch and listened intently. With every session her hunger to sing became stronger. This hunger, however, did not affect her ability. After quitting dance, guitar, modeling and trumpet, I felt it would be throwing money away and refused to provide voice lessons.

Aubry was determined. She found a way without me. She made a deal with the voice teacher. Aubry would babysit in trade for voice lessons. After the first lesson I assumed the teacher would inform the poor child she just can not sing and that would finally be the end of it! That was in 1987. Aubry has not missed a voice lesson in ten years. She now sings professionally. Her voice is like an angel's. I cry when I hear her sing. Partially because her voice is so beautiful but mostly because I have such pride in this little girl who never gave up on her dream until it became a reality. She was focused. She wanted it.

When people think they will never be able to sing. Aubry's teacher begins to play an audio cassette tape and then says, "Take a guess at who that is. That is Aubry Ludington's first lesson!" If you want it, you can have it. You just have to take action.

Becoming more humorous is just like becoming a great vocalist. You don't just wake up one morning and begin to laugh more. You have to do something about it. Be obsessive about it. Get fixed on the idea. Why don't you set a <u>laugh out loud goal</u> for yourself? Today, I am going to laugh out loud three times before I go home. The next day go for five times, then work your way up to ten laugh out louds a day. Now you have got to look for the funny! It helps to keep a journal. Start to write down everything that makes you laugh. This way you will begin to recognize what your type of humor is. It is true there are many different types of humor. Something that I find hysterical you may not even smile at and vice versa. Identify your funny bone, then look for the kinds of things that make you laugh.

Types of Humor
There are so many different types of humor.
Find out what you laugh at the most. Is it
slapstick? - The Three Stooges, Lucille Ball,
The Marx Brothers, Jim Carrey. Do you like
putdowns? - Don Rickles. Topical humor? -
Jay Leno, Dave Letterman, Bob Hope.
Impressions? -Rich Little. Props? - Carrot
Top. Characters? - Whoopie Goldberg, Lilly
Tomlin. How about the totally bizarre humor of
Stephen Wright? Or the flakiness of Gracie
Allen, Tommy Smothers or Goldie Hawn?
Spend some time finding out what makes you
laugh. Here are some examples of comedy that I
find funny.

Political Humor
"Liberals feel unworthy of their possessions...
Conservatives feel they deserve everything they've
stolen" - Mort Sahl

"Charles Manson appeared at his latest
parole hearing with a swastika carved into his
forehead...what better way to show the board
you're putting your act together?" - Dennis Miller

Observations
"Have you ever noticed that mice don't have
shoulders" - George Carlin

Comparisons
"My Father had three jobs and went to school
at night. If I go to the cleaners and the bank in
the same day...I need a nap!" - Larry Miller

Similes
Sex is like air - you don't miss it until you don't have it.

Music & Word Play
"Is Shelley Long or short?   Was John Gielgud Good all day?   What did Ernest Heming Weigh? Is Glenn Close?   Is Jamie Farr?   Did Tommie Tune his own guitar?   And What did Stevie Wonder?   - Dale Gonyea from his song Name Dropping

Absurdities
"I saw a stupid ad for a new improved microwave oven that can cook a meal in ten seconds. Are there really people who say, "Hey, "I've been home for ten seconds, where the hell is dinner?" - Jay Leno

Please excuse the penmanship as I am writing this in the shower - The letter was typed. - Woody Allen

Visualization & Imagery
"My mother in law is so large, one day she wore a gray dress and an admiral boarded her!" - Phyllis Diller

Relationships & Ironies
"Have you ever noticed how those Jehovah's Witnesses are always at your door?   Hey, I got a great idea. Why don't we let them deliver the mail?" - Gallagher

When I first started to work as a stand up comic, my good friend Bruno Schirripa, then owner of Wise Guys Comedy Club in Syracuse, New York, taught me that "a good comic thinks like a little kid." He's right. Stop and think about it. Little kids will laugh at anything. That's because they haven't been told not to. If we could just think the way little kids think, we would be able to find the funny side of life easily. So next Thanksgiving sit at the kids table and start to pay attention. You will be able to be really funny in a natural way.

A good way to find out what your type of humor is, is to start to keep a humor notebook. Include four sections. In the first section collect your favorite comic strips. They can come from anywhere: the newspaper, magazines, joke books or draw your own. The object is to find a picture and a caption that make you at least smile.

The second section will have your favorite jokes. Every time you hear a good joke write it down in your humor notebook. When you write something down it helps you to remember it better. This assignment may help you remember good jokes you can then retell at the next party. Here is a good one to get you started.

Joke

Two little kids take off all their clothes. The little girl stands up and the little boys stands on her head. He says, "Well, I'm on top of you. When is the fun gonna start?" She says, "I don't know but I've got a headache already."

In the third section of your humor notebook, begin a collection of word play. Begin to collect newspaper headlines that crack you up.

Example: *"Man killed in scramble over eggs."* Find signs or advertisements that make you laugh. This silly sign was on our bulletin board at work: *Dog for sale. Eats anything. Especially fond of children.* Or find bumper stickers that make you smile, *"Don't follow me, I'm lost."* I loved this one: *Columbus did not know where he was going. When he got back he didn't know where he'd been. And he did it all on borrowed money. There's hope for all of us."* Fill this section with quotes, one liners, epigrams, aphorisms, sayings or observations. You are looking for anything that combines wit with wisdom. Here are a few examples:

✓ First it was the handicapped spot now it's the pregnant mother spot. How about a stupid person spot for those of us who can never find our car.

✓ Why do we park in the driveway and drive on the parkway?

✓ Why do we call dwellings that are stuck together, apartments?

Oxymorons

cruel kindness - are you cruel in a kind way?
or kind of cruel
pre board - are you boarding before you board?
water landing - is it water or land?
near miss - did you miss it or almost hit it?
death benefit - and the benefit..."
jumbo shrimp - is it large or is it small?
human intelligence - O.K. not the ones I've dated!

Malapropisms

Bacteria...The back door of a cafeteria
Cesarean Section...A neighborhood in Rome
CAT Scan...Searching for Kitty
Dilate...To live long
Morbid...a higher offer

In your last section write down three of your favorite stand up comics. If you don't have three favorites it would be a good idea to start renting videos that introduce you to the acts of stand up comics. Find people that you think are just hysterical. They can be hot new comics or age old favorites. From Lucy or Jack Benny to Robin Williams. Anyone who makes you laugh should go in this section. Try to find a tape of the work of these comedians. Really pay attention to the type of humor they do. The more you find out about what they do that makes you laugh, the easier it will be for you to understand your own sense of humor. Now it should be much easier for you to find the funny side of life.

For those of you who are thinking, "I just don't like stand up comedy.", could you force yourself this one time? The only way to break old habits is to form new ones. Get in the habit of watching and enjoying stand up comedy just for this exercise. You will be able to realize your own style of humor and begin to see the funnier side of life. Just as in any other goal setting situation, you have to try. I realize this will have you stepping outside of your comfort zone at times. Trust me that is a good thing.

EXERCISE #6

What's So Funny?

Exercise: Humor survey

Note your favorite funny person/situation in each category. Why are they your favorite?

TV Shows _____

_____

Movies _____

_____

Jokes _____

_____

Friend _____

_____

Boss _____

_____

Co-Worker _____

_____

Neighbor _____

_____

Priest/minister/rabbi _____

_____

Doctor _____

_____

Store clerk _____

_____

Sales experience _____

_____

Restaurant experience _____

_____

What If I Don't Feel Like Laughing?

When we are in a bad mood the last thing we want to hear is, "Cheer up!" That really is great advice, however, do not give people advice unless you are asked. Socrates went around giving people advice and they poisoned him. It is important to understand what we can do about the mood we are in. Think of a bad mood as a cancer in the human body. Left unattended, that bad mood just spreads. If we don't find a way to eliminate it, a bad mood can lead to depression and serious mental illness. We must have an action plan. Put together some specific steps to take when ever we feel sad, lonely, depressed or just not ourself. Follow the pan. When I feel blue I take out my Bill Cosby tape and begin to laugh. Sometimes a nice refreshing walk outside will do the trick.

Did you ever go to the gym and exercise even though you really didn't feel like exercising? Did you get the benefits of the exercise anyway? Did you feel more energized after you finished? Did you still tone your muscles and burn calories even though you really didn't feel like exercising? Sure you did! That is the same thing that happens when you don't feel like laughing, but you laugh or smile anyway. Try it and see for yourself. When things are not what you would want them to be and people are not treating you the way you think they should and traffic is just not running the way it should be running, that is when you need to force yourself to find the funny! Force that laugh and smile to come through. I promise you that you will reap the benefits of humor even though you don't feel like it! Sometimes I just go into my room, close the door and have a laugh festival. I laugh hysterically for a good five minutes. It is a great way to wake up if you're sitting at the desk half asleep. Laughing is the greatest pick me up. You don't really even have to have anything to laugh about. Just think of it as exercise.

We've already talked about the physical benefits of laughter; our blood pressure drops, heart rate lowers and generally promotes good health. I have found that laughter and humor also promote teamwork, build confidence, encourage problem solving, prevent burnout, reduce fear, stimulate creativity, elevate moods and helps us become more productive. Humor brings people together.

Let's learn from our experiences not to be broken by them. It's the same whether we are at work or at home or in the grocery store. We can let our problems over burden us and allow stress and worry to destroy us or we can learn to cope using a wonderful tool - our sense of humor. It is simply a matter of choice.

Humor Skills

Humor is a skill and it requires daily repetition and practice. What is the one thing we have control over? Our actions or the way in which we respond to any given situation. We have the power of choice. We can either choose to use the skills or choose to find an excuse not to.

Even if you recognize what makes you laugh, how will that improve your humor skills, you say? Easy. Open up your eyes, ears, nose and all of your senses. Be ready to find the funny. Your sense of humor is simply your ability to see the absurdity in difficult situations. I find that my most stressful situation is behind the wheel of my car. I'm always on a mission, everyone else is on vacation. I always get behind the guy who likes to slow down for the garage sale, but never quite pulls over and goes to the garage! The worst situation is when I'm stuck in a traffic jam. I have a real problem with sitting and doing nothing, I always have to be accomplishing something. (My therapist says this stems from my childhood when someone must have continually told me to hurry up .. I don't recall who.) I have been known to paint all ten nails perfectly, while listening to books on tape and riding along the New York State Thruway.

To be sure that I don't boil over, should I get stuck in traffic. I keep my stress buster in the glove compartment. To occupy the time while I sit waiting for traffic to resume, I put on my red sponge clown nose and wait for the driver next to me to see me and react. Sometimes, if I'm on the Garden State Parkway, it takes a while before anyone looks at me. Then when they do, some still don't laugh, so I put on my Smile on a Stick. That usually gets them laughing. I do this because it makes me laugh. It passes the time without getting me all worked up about accomplishing nothing. I have accomplished something. I've made someone laugh who probably was as stressed out as I was. It works.

I know some of you may think this is not what normal people do. You're right, but who wants to be normal? Never forget that only the dead fish swim <u>with</u> the stream! Remember what Shakespeare said, "Things are neither good nor bad but thinking makes it so." So if you think being a bit wacky will help you through the day, it will. You can be different! You can be creative. You can get wacky. You can go bananas. It works!

Your humor skills are your ability to take yourself lightly while you take your work seriously. Put a little zip into your step. Spread some joy around the office. Giggle, smile for no reason, be happy.

Think about it. Who is your dentist? Your doctor? Where do you go for coffee? What is your favorite restaurant? Your favorite club? Who is your dry cleaner? Are these places that you choose to go filled with grumpy, hateful, annoyed people. I don't think so. You wouldn't go there. An ancient Chinese Proverb says, "A person without a smiling face must not open a shop!" It makes sense. We frequent places where people make us feel good. Places where people give us a smile, remember our name, maybe even say something nice to us. These are the places that we return to. I have my morning coffee at The Tivoli on Park Avenue in Rochester, New York. This adorable little cafe is filled with the smell of freshly baked pastries and dark brewed coffee. The coffee is too strong for me so I have to dilute it with water. It is also a bit pricey and I don't eat fat filled pastries. Why then, would I go there every morning for overpriced strong coffee? Because the sweet little Italian lady who works there loves me! Or at least she has convinced me that she loves me. I walk in and she hugs me and tells me I look beautiful. I need that more than coffee some mornings. She asks me where I'm going that day. She notices if I miss a few days and wants to know where I've been. She asks about my children and my sisters and my mom. I noticed that she does this with everyone but I like to think I'm special and she just likes me. It's a great way to begin my day on a high note and with a smile.

On my way to Lake Placid, New York to do a workshop for Time Warner Cable, I stopped for gas near Fort Drum on Route 342. A young man approximately twenty-five years old met me as I parked in front of the pump. Full of energy and smiles he said, "Hi. What can I do for you this morning?" I told him to fill it up and asked to use the ladies room. "Yes ma'am" he said with enthusiasm, "Right around the corner but please excuse the mess. We just opened and I still have lots of work to do in there!" When I returned he had washed all my windows and was just finishing pumping gas. "$10.08 please." Then he said "I'm so happy. This is the happiest I've ever been. I just can't wait to go to work in the morning." Noticing the Grand Opening banner stretched across the front of the building I said. "You must be the proud new owner!" "Yes ma'am and I love this work. Talking to people and helping them. Why I got $7.00 in tips today! Can you believe it?" "Yes I can" I said as I drove away. "Yes I can." When was the last time you tipped your gas station attendant? I never have. However, this guy was so full of energy and joy I could understand how he had managed to be so fortunate. I could tell how happy he was by the warm smile he greeted me with. It was obvious he was there to help his customers and make them feel special. With that attitude his new business will do just fine.

A happy heart makes the face cheerful.
Proverbs 17:22.

I do my banking at a small branch office near my home. When I go in I almost always get the same teller, Gladys Griffin. A cheerful young woman, who has a knack for finding something fun and uplifting to say to me every time. It doesn't matter if it's Wednesday at 2:00 pm and I'm the only one in line or if it's Friday afternoon at 4:00 pm and eight people are huffing and puffing, she always has a smile and always treats me like I'm her only customer. She really went out of the way a few months ago when she sent me a thank you note in the mail for being such a nice customer! I couldn't believe it!

We go where we are made to feel special. We go where we have fun. We do business with people who make us feel better. If you smiled more, laughed more, were in a better mood, do you think it would change your day? What would it do for how valuable you are at work? Try it. What have you got to lose? My dentist cracks jokes while he works on my teeth and that's why I go to him.

Right now sit down and make a list of all the places where you do business. How many of them are places where the people, for the most part, are pleasant and cheerful? See, I told you it works!

You can choose to find something to smile or laugh about or you can choose to be annoyed by things that happen every day. It's up to you what kind of atmosphere you work in. It's up to you how situations turn out. You can control your own response.

Here's a perfect example of a situation that could have been annoying. I settled down for a flight from Rochester to Chicago in an aisle seat of a crowded plane. The heavy set man across the aisle got up to put his coat in the overhead compartment as a line of passengers waited to find their seats. He took his jacket off and unknowingly hit me in the face with the sleeve as he swung it up into the compartment above. Then he bent over to move something out of his seat just as I turned to look his way. His butt was eye level with and maybe an inch from my nose!   I chuckled to myself and as my eyes moved forward I saw six people in line all chuckling right along with me. They passed by and one man leaned over and whispered with a smile, "I bet that just made your day!"

On another flight from Fort Myers to Charlotte a petite flight attendant with a cheerful smile seemed to have something nice to say to everyone with whom she came into contact. I commented that I noticed how pleasant she was and told her I appreciated it. She said, "I love my job!" "Well it shows", I replied.

Do what you love and you'll love what you're doing!

<u>Who Is My Customer?</u>

• The customer is the most important person in our business.

• The customer is not dependent on us, we are dependent on the customer.

• The customer is not an interruption of our work; but the purpose of it.

• The customer does us an honor when calling on us. We are not doing him a favor by serving him/her.

• The customer is part of our business, not an outsider.

• The customer is our guest.

• The customer is not a cold statistic, but flesh and blood; a human with feelings and emotions like our own.

• The customer is not someone to argue with or match wits with.

• The customer is one who brings us his/her wants. Our job is to fill them.

• The customer is deserving of the most courteous and attentive treatment we can provide.

• The customer has the right to expect an employee to present a neat, clean appearance.

EXERCISE #7

This Is My Customer

Create four different types of people who may come to you for service or products. Describe a customer: gender, approximate age, family situation, income level. Who might come to buy with them? Why would they come to you over someone else?

#1 _____

_____

_____

_____

#2 _____

_____

_____

_____

#3 _____

_____

_____

_____

#4 _____

_____

_____

_____

Chapter Seven
Humor Tools For
Successful Living

"He has achieved success who has lived well,
laughed often, and loved much,"
-Bessie Anderson Stanley

I'm an avid user of tools. The dictionary says that a tool is something we use to shape, form, or finish with. Humor tools are there to help us shape and form our day which will make a big difference in how that day shapes up, forms, or finishes!

Some of these ideas may seem outrageous or uncomfortable to you. "I'm not in the habit of acting silly!" you say? Well, it's time to change your habits! If you always do what you've always done, then you'll always get what you've always got...Unless you make a conscious decision to change some aspect of your life, you will continue the way you are indefinitely. Research tells us that if we do something 21 days in a row we will form a new habit. Take the Humor Habit Challenge. For 21 days use at least three of the following humor tools and see how your habits change. Just think of how much happier you will be. Allow me to introduce to you some of the humor tools that I use on a regular basis.

Mini Vacation

Some offices have Friday Dress Down Day. This is a mini vacation away from having to put on pantyhose and ties for just one day! That's the whole idea. Encourage your office to have a 70's day when everyone comes in dressed in polyester and bell bottoms. Silly Hat Day when everyone has to bring in and wear a goofy hat all day long. Have a supply of hats on hand to assign to people who forgot to bring one. Make sure the ones in the extra supply box are really obnoxious ones! You can't be upset with someone who looks goofy. Have accent day everyone has to talk with an accent. Trust me you'll be laughing all day long. The best is Elvis Day everyone comes in bloated and the boss treats everyone with peanut butter and banana sandwiches at noon.

At home you can have mini vacations too. The idea is just to get you away from the situation you are in for just a brief time and change the atmosphere. I remember when I was a kid on Sunday we all had to dress up all day long. Mom set the dining room table with linens and china. She was always a great cook but on Sunday she made sure everything was special. I remember she even had crystal candle holders and long white candles that we got to blow out at the end of the meal. After the dishes were done we usually went for a ride. Who goes for a ride anymore? Mom and Dad rode up front and all four of us girls squashed in the back seat of Dad's 1959 Cadillac. We could barely see out of the windows, but we didn't care. We were going for a ride! We would drive way out into the country and Dad would look for some people sitting on their front porch. He would then pull into their driveway, toot the horn and we'd all stick our heads out of the window and yell, "We're here!" The people would get up and look at us trying to figure out who we were. At that point, Dad would back out of the driveway and continue down the road. We laughed for miles.

We were taking a mini vacation from our everyday life. Mom was away from the kitchen. Dad was out of the office. The girls and I were away from school for just a few hours having fun with each other and making memories. We did that almost every Sunday. It was a great way for all of us to begin our new week fresh and relaxed.

EXERCISE #8
Mini Vacation

Come up with five things that you can do today that would be different than how you normally do things. When you do something different it's like taking a mini vacation away from your normal day. A change of pace...new scenery...new faces...fresh air...all these things can make a big difference in how you feel. Small changes can make big differences.

From 6:30 a.m. to 5:00 p.m.
Example:
I'm going to take a different route to work!
I'm going to eat my lunch with chop sticks!

1. _____
2. _____
3. _____
4. _____
5. _____

From 6:00p.m. to 11:00p.m.
Example:
Tonight we are going to eat together as a family in the dining room!

After dinner we are all going for a ride in the country - the whole family!

1. _____
2. _____
3. _____
4. _____
5. _____

Be Someone Famous

When you are at wits end and just totally out of control, stop and think, "What would Erma Bombeck or Robin Williams do in this situation?"

Complaint Tank

Have co-workers put all their work problems in the complaint tank. At the Monday morning meeting, break into groups and have each group take a problem. Make this a contest to see which group comes up with the best solution. Now everyone has a hand in correcting the problems.

The Pep Talk

Choose three people in your life whom you know, love and respect you. Make sure these are people who believe that what you do is important. These will be your PTP, Pep Talk People. Keep your PTP phone numbers in your wallet. When ever you are having a bad day or you just think you can't take another minute, call one of your pep talk people. They will remind you of your successes. They will put you back on track and help you to keep going. If you choose these people wisely they will have a laugh or two for you on the way.

The Humor Prescription

When someone in your office is going through a hard time surprise them with a prescription for relief. Write out something fun for a friend or co-worker to do in the form of a medical prescription. Example: Tell two jokes and see me in the morning. Make a Humor Pill Bottle. Take an empty pill bottle and fill it with bits of paper with fun things to do on them.

License to Laugh

Use customized license plates "OK2SMILE" Or "IMHAPPY". Every time you get into your car, you are reminded that you are happy and it is O.K. to smile. It also tells everyone else that it is O.K. to smile.

Clown Ring

Use as your secret serious decoder ring. Wear it on your pinky when ever you have to go to a stuffy meeting or be with stiff people.

Motivational Cards

When you feel like the cards are stacked against you, change decks! Inspirational quotes will help you to become a better you!

The Joy List

The most important gift you can give yourself is a Joy List. This list consists of everything and anything that brings you any amount of Joy! The smell of fresh flowers, a child's smile, a green light or finding money on the ground (I personally love this one). My list only had four things on it when I first started it. Now it has three full pages. Begin with the most precious, the people in your life, and then move on to nature and music and literature. Soon you too will have pages and pages of joy to reflect on. Now take this list out and re-read it when ever you need to remind yourself of all the things that you have that bring joy into your life. Be thankful.

John Kennedy Jr. said, "To whom much is given, much is expected". He may have been referring to his great wealth. However, his quote should have meaning for all of us, regardless of our financial status. This list of all the things we have been given, helps us realize all that we have to be thankful for. It motivates us to accomplish more, to be better parents, children, sisters, brothers and friends. When you count your blessings, it makes you want to be better at everything you do.

When you find yourself all tense and overworked, take a five minute Joy Break. Pick something off your list to enjoy for just five minutes. Don't be so busy doing that you can no longer enjoy being! If you are so busy trying to be a success that you have a short Joy List, remember that success is measured by the degree that you are enjoying peace, health, love and joy in your life. Sit down right now and write down ten things that make you joyful.

You can't get started? Here is my first list: My three sisters, my mother, my father, my children, ...and now a few off of my current list! #7 Lazy Sunday mornings, #12 The smell of fresh coffee, #18 Finding money, #42 Getting a manicure, #70 Spring rain.

Ask every member of the family to make a Joy List. You will be surprised to learn what is really meaningful to them. This helps you to better understand each family member and what makes them happy.

EXERCISE #9
Joy List

The Joy List will change your life. On this list goes everything that brings Joy into your life. From sunshine to a strangers smile - put anything that makes you smile, feel warm and fuzzy, and just plain happy on this list.

Example of what can go on your list:

Seinfeld Reruns	Old Three Stooges Movies
Spring Flowers	Paid Holidays
Rebates	Free Samples
My faith	Walks in the summer
Sunshine	The smell of sauce simmering

Begin your list and remember to add to it whenever you think of something that brings you joy. You now have a list you can refer to at a moments notice to remind yourself of all that you have to be thankful for.

The wonderful thing about the Joy List is that it can be the very thing to fall back on when the going gets tough!

Example: Suppose having to have dinner with a co-worker is on my Woe is Me list and the smell of fresh simmering tomato sauce and going to a play is on my Joy List. Maybe combining the two will soften the stress factor and sort of balance out the evening.

My kids are having a slumber party and the constant giggling is driving me crazy. I plan ahead and rent four old Three Stooges Movies and what do you know...I've made it through the night without stress!

EXERCISE #9
My Joy List

_____
_____
_____
_____
_____
_____
_____
_____
_____
_____
_____
_____
_____
_____
_____
_____

Unorthodox Party

Have a beach party in the middle of winter. Fill a kiddie pool with water and have beach balls floating around. Everyone wears summer clothes and straw hats and you serve summer fun foods like watermelon and iced tea. This is a great way to get out of the winter blahs for one afternoon.

Monday Morning Joke Line

Monday morning at 8:00 start a joke line network. Have one person start the chain with a joke. Each person calls their chain partner with the week's joke. This is a great way to start off the week.

First Aid Giggle Kits

Every family and every office should have a first aid giggle kit. You may add anything to your giggle kit that will make you laugh or smile or just relax. The whole purpose of the kit is to take you away for a moment. It's there to help you to relax enough so that when you do get back to the situation at hand, you'll have a clear head and be ready to focus and be productive.

Some people who have attended my workshops have included pictures of their children or other loved ones in the giggle kits. I think that is an excellent idea because it reminds us quickly of what's important in our lives. Another entertaining idea is to have silly pictures of other co-workers available!

Sometimes we tend to get to the boiling point so quickly that we need a device that will bring things back into proper perspective. We often need something to help us to step back a moment and see the situation a bit more clearly. Giggle kits are great to send to kids in college or to a friend who has moved to a new city and is feeling alone. It is a great way to put a smile on anyone's face. Here are a few more ideas you may want to include in your giggle kit: • Small hand held games • Checkers • Bubbles • Silly Toys • Gum/Candy • Joke Books • Small Inspirational Books • Poems • Short Stories • Cassette Tapes of Comedians • Videos of Comedians • Baby Pictures of Co-Workers • Silly Headlines

Take a New Route to the Office

Just for the heck of it, go the long way to work. Stop at a different coffee shop tomorrow morning. Instead of having your regular black coffee, have a hot chocolate instead. In other words do something different. The change of pace will be good for you. Keep your life full of surprises.

Friday Afternoon Party.

One company I worked for used to have pizza and soda for everyone in the cafeteria every Friday afternoon! It was a great way to end the week and a nice way to get to know my co-workers.

Red Sponge Clown Nose

Great to use when stuck in a traffic jam. Just put on your nose and wait for the person next to you to notice and watch the fun begin and the stress end. Also a great way to halt little silly spats around the house. No one can be mad at a clown!

Silly Head Band
Wear this on a bad hair day. Everyone will be looking at the head band and not at your hair so you have nothing to worry about. Use it when you need to feel like a King or Queen! Wear it like a crown! Better yet - wear a crown!

Standing Ovation
Give someone a standing ovation for just being there. This is your opportunity to let someone know you appreciate them everyday, not just when they do something extraordinary

Think Like a Child
Children have boundless energy. Laughter, joy and playfulness comes natural to them and help create an atmosphere where creativity just thrives.

Keep pictures of yourself when you were a child on your desk. Choose the one that shows you having the most fun. This will remind you to stay young and keep the kid in you alive.

No Reason Surprises
For no reason at all do something for someone at the office. One of my co-workers once put a small vase with one rosebud on her friend's desk with a note that said, "This bud's for you!". It makes you feel so good when you do something for someone else. Be creative. Make a fun coupon for a free coffee or candy bar and give it to someone.

Socialize

Have one fun thing to do each month with the office crew. Schedule specific dates for a night at the comedy club, going to the movies together, go cart racing or roller skating . By doing these fun activities with the people you work with on a regular basis, you create relationships. When people are friends they get along better and they work better with one another. Have a "social savings" that is funded by the ones that need the fun the most. Every time someone in the office is negative or angry about something, they have to toss in a buck! This will help defer the cost of the monthly fun trips.

Cartoon Rewrite

When you need to stimulate your creative muscles, sit down and try to think of several new captions for a cartoon! Use this as a fun game to take you away from a problem just long enough to clear your mind and help you to think more clearly.

Using cartoon rewrites is a great way to start a meeting on a high note.

Go back to the cartoons you have in your humor notebook. White out the captions and pass them around before a Monday morning meeting. Ask your co-workers to work in teams to think up new captions for each cartoon. You may use any picture. Find one in a newspaper or magazine or bring one in from home. Or use the ones on the following pages. This is a great way to start a meeting because it promotes teamwork, it gets you thinking in unorthodox ways and it's fun so everyone gets involved. By

beginning to think creatively and in an
unorthodox way you're better equipped to come
up with creative solutions for that real challenge
you're facing.

EXERCISE #10
Create A Caption

#1 _____

#2 _____

#3 _____

#4 _____

#5 _____

A. Cerullo

Create A Caption

#1 _____

#2 _____

#3 _____

#4 _____

#5 _____

Create A Caption

#1 _____

#2 _____

#3 _____

#4 _____

#5 _____

Create A Caption

#1 _____

#2 _____

#3 _____

#4 _____

#5 _____

EXERCISE #11
Cartoon Re-Write

Creativity begins by having fun! When we are having fun, we are more alert, less worried about what others will think of our ideas. After all, it's just for fun! This is a wonderful exercise to do at the beginning of a meeting. It helps us to think outside the lines - out of the box! Do not judge your thoughts. Just put everything that comes to mind down on paper. You will be surprised with what you come up with.

Create a picture for the following or make up some captions of your own.

I should have known!

Is that all there is?

Not again!

EXERCISE #12

Let's Get Together. Yeah Yeah Yeah!

Nothing brings a group of people together like a good hearty laugh! Having fun together is your best tool for building a great working team. Think of ways to do just that both at work and at home.

Team building exercise:

Example:

Once a month our office will go to a comedy club together as a group. Create a joke box. Everyone has to drop one good clean joke into the box and at the end of the work week we share pizza, Cokes and jokes! At home we all go to the video store and vote on the funniest movie to rent or rent several and go home and laugh together all night!

Develop three team building strategies for your company

1._____

_____

2._____

_____

3._____

_____

Develop three team building strategies for your family.

1._____

_____

2._____

_____

3._____

_____

Outside The Box Thinking

In this creative problem solving exercise list as many uses as you can for some simple, everyday object. Example: <u>Tea Bag Usage.</u> Participants of my workshop were able to think up many ways to use a tea bag! By the time they were finished with this exercise they were ready to solve real problems in a creative way.

Here are some ideas participants have come up with. You could use a tea bag as a noise maker for quiet people, back pack for mice, makeup remover pad, Christmas tree ornament, car air freshener, pot pourri, eye soother, cat nip, breast soother for nursing mom, garland, inexpensive toy for kids, dental floss, stuffing for pillows, pillow for hamster, pillow for Barbie, baby bean bag, hot water heating pad for mice, pin cushion, frisbee, perfume, dye, wobbly chair fixer, door jam, dusting rag, aroma therapy, tissue, eye glass cleaner, eye make up remover, reminder (use string to tie around your finger), ring, cow manure in a play farm set, business card for Juan Valdez, compost pile, sponge to wash the car, seat cushion for a doll with hemorrhoids, confetti at a wedding, nose bleed stopper, nail polish remover pad, drawer sachet, door stop for doll house, mixed with lotion for facial scrub, base for mice little league, butterfly mattress, toe separator for pedicure, compress, sponge, toss a cross bean bag, bug crusher, heal support in shoes, sprinkle on ice for traction, teddy bear hat, empty & use bag as diaper for dolly, squeeze for stress relief, perspiration absorber, good luck charm, earrings, cat toy, ear plugs, hacky sack, use as fuzzy dice, as an eye

patch, to relieve a swollen eye, wear it as a pin,
play hopscotch with it, life preserver for a fly,
make a tea mobile, patch for bunions, use tea
leaves to tell fortunes, kitty litter, padding for a
breakable gift.

Bird Calls On Hold

My friend Bernie Nonenmacher told me about
a seed company that has birds chirping on hold
rather than the music on hold that most
companies have. She said is was such a pleasant
change from the norm.

Be Spontaneous

As president of the Breakfast Brokers Tip
Exchange Club I felt it was my responsibility to
keep the group upbeat and positive and continue
to energize the 7:30 am meeting. On this
particular morning I noticed a large furry head in
the waitress station. Curious, I went right in and
took a closer look. It was one of those full head
masks from a gorilla suit! Perfect! Someone had
left it behind. I guess you could say he lost his
head! I asked the waitress if I could borrow it
for my morning meeting.

The Breakfast Brokers, a gathering of 25 to
30 people from various types of businesses, meet
once a week and exchange tips or information
about what is happening in the community. We
often would invite prospective members to a
meeting. The perspective member would tell a
bit about himself and his business and how he
feels he could contribute to the club.

On this morning as soon as everyone got
seated I opened the meeting and told them I had

a guest coming who I thought would be a great asset to us. His name was Mr. Tony Grillo and he was opening a chain of banana stands all over the city. As I told of the advantages, I was laughing inside at the confused look on their faces. "This is going to be the replacement of coffee houses and we are right here at the very beginning of the new trend. Just think of it. The ability to drive up to the drive through and get a nice bowl of fresh bananas for your mid morning break!" I warned them to be very professional as he is a very wealthy newcomer from South Africa and I wanted him to have a good impression of us. I teased that I thought he was a bit of a party animal at heart and thought he would fit right in with our group!

As the members began to adjust their ties and sit up nice and straight I excused myself to go out in the hall and get our guest. I then proceeded to put the hairy black gorilla head on over my business suit and burst into the room shaking hands and greeting everyone! I jumped up on the chairs and made the sounds of a gorilla, scratched under my arms and jumped up and down. At first they were so startled they didn't know what to think. Then little by little each one realized they'd been had by the president! The laughter was thunderous! Some people actually had tears running down their faces they were laughing so hard. Once in a while it's good to be totally wacky.

Make a habit of adding outrageous acts to your daily routine. Wear "Jackie O" sun glasses and sit at a coffee bar and pretend you are her.

If you're feeling really great one morning "call

in well". Call it your, "Mental Health Day". Take
the day off and go enjoy yourself. Make faces in
the mirror daily. Stick out your tongue at
unexpected moments. Next time you get into an
elevator, just for fun, face the rear. Do something
nice for a stranger. Pay for the guy in the car
behind you at a toll booth. Have a group of your
friends stand together and get everyone to point
and look up for no reason. See how many
people you can get to join you out of pure
wonder! Sometimes take things literally and do
exactly what you are told. Drop everything. Be
silly. The next time someone really annoys you go
home and bake a whole batch of gingerbread
men and bite off the heads.

Don't just do things because *that's the way
they've always been done.* Find out why it's
always been done that way. If you can find a
better way, don't be afraid to try it. Be a pioneer.
Do something totally new and different. And
speaking of different I offer the Ham Story...

A little girl was watching her mom cook
Sunday dinner when she noticed her mother cut
off what seemed to be a perfectly good slice of
ham and throw it away. "Mom why did you cut
off the end of the ham?" Her mother replied, "I
don't know. My mom always cut the end off the
ham before she cooked it." Not satisfied with the
answer the little girl asked her grandmother why
she always cut the end off the ham before she
cooked it. "Because my mother always did it that
way." the grandmother answered. The next day
when she visited her granny she asked her why
she had always cut the end off her ham before
she put it in the oven to cook. The old woman

simply replied, "because my child, my pot was too small!" When someone says that's the way it's always been done, be sure and ask why!

"In the end what truly counts can only be measured in songs sung and bread shared, in bodies healed and minds liberated, in faithful work done and joyful risks taken, in great gladness of heart and in His name being praised!" - This quote was taken from the Asbury Methodist church flyer on the very Sunday that I was writing this chapter! Take risks. Sing songs. Share. Be faithful. Be joyful. And by all means...Praise His Holy Name!

YVONNE CONTE

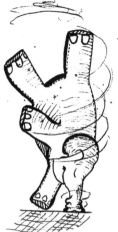

Chapter Eight
Creative Fun Things To Do

"Be brave enough to live creatively. The creative is the place where no one else has ever been. You have to leave the city of your comfort and go into the wilderness of your intuition. You can't get there by bus, only by hard work, risking, and by not quite knowing what you're doing. What you'll discover will be wonderful: yourself."
- Alan Alda

Hopefully you will have found something here that inspires you to take action towards a more laughter filled life. Even though a lot of the ideas in this book may seem silly at first, they really do have long term positive results. By sitting down to do something fun and different with people at work or at home, you are getting your creative juices moving. This allows you to start thinking "out of the box" without judging and that is the way to come up with real solutions to real problems. You are also able to see things differently which helps you to look at all possible solutions not just yours. This helps you to communicate and understand one another. And last but certainly not least, you are laughing together. Laughing together brings people together. It makes everything so much easier. So the next time you are faced with all the things you **should** be doing, take a deep breath and think of some of the things you **could** be doing!

In the end what it really boils down to is you. How do you want to live your life? Do you want to take the steps to add humor and laughter to your day? Is it worth it to you? It must be or you would never have made it all the way to this chapter of the book. So here you go. These are some ideas I've used with my children as they were growing up that made it fun to be a mom and made for great memories. It's not the expensive sneakers you buy or don't buy for your kids that matters, it's the simple fun times that you share with them. The memories of laughter and shared family time - that's just plain GOLD!

✓ **Theme dinner -**

Choose a theme, just like high schools do for prom night. Build your evening around the theme. Here is a great example: I remember one afternoon I invited my good friend Linda Carpenter and her three children over for dinner. When I called to invite her, I spoke in a southern accent and pretended I was Scarlet O'Hara inviting her to Tara. We spoke in southern accents all day. I spent hours putting my hair in long ringlets and wore a beautiful red dress and lots of flashy jewels! We had black eyed peas and cornbread and southern fried chicken. We video taped our dinner and still laugh when we get to the part when Linda looked at the table set so pretty and said, "Oh my Scarlett, I love what you've done with this place during the war and everything!" This is a fun way to spend an afternoon and everyone can get into the act.

✓ **Backwards dinner -**
Begin with dessert and then your main course and then your salad or soup. It's just a different and fun way to have dinner some night.

✓ **Write a country western song about your family -**
The song has to include: a pick up truck, railroad tracks, a dog, your mother, drinking and a broken heart or two.

✓ **Put on a play at home for no reason -**
Keep a box of old clothes and props that you can get into at a moments notice. Encourage family members to make up a play as you go along. Act out a nursery rhyme or a song. Improvise! The times I cherish most began the summer of 1977. Carolyn Williams and I sat on the front porch swing of our rented duplex and watched our children entertain us. Aubry, Johnny, and Carolyn's twins, David and Angie used their impressive imaginations and a few props that summer to put on variety shows. As we drank our cups

of coffee, they became anyone or anything their little hearts desired. It was the best of times.

✓ Clown around dinner -

Instead of telling your children to sit up straight and mind your manners, how about letting them express themselves? You may learn something about each other that you would have never even imagined. Give every member of the family a clown nose. They must wear it at the table during dinner. You will be laughing all night with this idea.

✓ Have an Affair -

I know you are wondering about this one. I mean have an affair with your spouse. Pretend! Meet at a secret place. Don't tell anyone except your spouse. Make up pretend names to call each other. Do secret things like meet for lunch at a motel. Be your husband's mistress. Be your wife's romantic love.

✓ Trade Places -

You sit and watch cartoons on Saturday morning and let the kids make breakfast.

✓ "Sing Only" Hour -

Make it a requirement that everyone sing whatever they need to say for one hour. Absolutely no talking! Only singing. This one is a riot. Especially if you get company or the phone rings during the hour.

✓ Shop Like Julia Roberts -

Go shopping at the most expensive shop in town. Try on ten of the most expensive outfits they have. Just for the pure fun of it.

✓ Top Ten List -

A wonderful way to pass the time while riding in the car is to pick a topic and write a top ten list much like David Letterman's famous list. You will smile for miles.

✓ America's Funniest Video tapes -

Even if you don't win the $10,000 this will be great fun for the entire family and you will have funny videos to watch for years to come. This is also a great idea for the office. Nothing brings a team together quicker then a fun project like this. Ask your department to create a funny commercial about your company. You may end up using it to promote business. If the office video wins think of the free publicity you could get for your business!

✓ 4th of July Costume Party -

On the fourth of July while the neighbors are having the traditional picnic, do something a little more exciting. Dress up like Betsy Ross, The Liberty Bell or Statue of Liberty. At the party, make all the food red, white or blue! You will be surprised how much fun you will begin to have if you just try something different once in a while. Be brave. Break the mold.

✓ Bingo or charades -

Playing these games with friends and family members makes for great fun. By including all members, young and old, it really brings people together.

✓ Special Occasion Night -

Some night when it is not a special occasion - make one! Prepare something different for dinner. Light the candles! Play soft music. Put the cat and the kids out. Hang the do not disturb sign on the door. Unplug the phone. Get crazy!!

✓ Helping hands dinner -

Every member of the family has to make a part of the dinner. With everyone involved there is a feeling of connection right from the beginning. It is not just the same old pot roast.

✓ Christmas Gag Gifts -

Every Christmas exchange Gag Gifts. Try to put a lot of thought into these gifts to make them as appropriate as possible. One year my plumber brother-in-law got a, "say no to crack" poster. It was a picture of a plumber bending over and his crack was showing. My sister hung it in a frame over their bed for years.

✓ Card Contest -

Go to a good card store and read the funny cards. See who can find the funniest card in the store.

✓ Christmas Card Classics -

Take a whole roll of film of your family making the funniest faces possible. Choose the one that makes you laugh the most to use as your Christmas Card. If it made you laugh, it will make all your friends and relatives laugh too. What a nice present that would be to give someone a good laugh!

✓ Fun Phone Message -

Come up with a creative fun message for your home answer machine. Examples: "Hello This is Bob Dole. Bob Dole is not home right now..." or "This is the Foreman Home. For George, press 1. For George, press 2. For George, press 3." Or "You have reached Martha Stewart's Home, While you are on hold why not make a flower vase out of your phone receiver? Just unscrew the top portion and fill with water..."

✓ Adult Peter Pan Birthday Party -

Use children's birthday toys for an adult birthday party. It feels great to be young again and to have as much fun as the kids do. Try it! Even Margaret Mead thinks it's a good idea. She said, "I was wise enough to never grow up while fooling most people into believing I had." On Dad's 84th birthday we all wore silly pointed children's hat's.

"Fun doesn't depend on money or status or circumstances of your life. Fun is ultimately a state of mind" - Unknown

22 Ways to Ruin a Bad Day

Plant a flower

Wash your car

Play the piano

Use the fine china

Over tip the waitress

Buy yourself flowers

Count your blessings

Return a borrowed item

Watch a beautiful sunset

Watch a beautiful sunrise

Smile at a negative person

Listen to your favorite music

Begin by singing in the shower

Buy a candy bar for a co-worker

Call your funniest friend for lunch

Make faces at yourself in a mirror

Pack your lunch with a cloth napkin

Put money in expired parking meters

Be the first to say "Hello" to a stranger

Put a lottery ticket inside your loved ones pocket

Send a note to an elderly relative just to say "Hello!"

Wave at children in the back seat of the car in front of you

Chapter Nine
Making Memories

*There is no better feeling than to look back on
your life with the fondest of memories.*
- Yvonne Conte

It is so important to create good memories for
your children. One way to do this is to share
stories with them of the funny things that have
happened in your family. Tell these memories
and anecdotes of yours over and over . Do it for
yourself and as a legacy for your children. Start
a new tradition at holiday time to come to
holiday dinner with a funny story to share about
a family member past or present.

Not That Kind Of Farm
by
Fran Block

I married a young man who's father ran the
pharmacy in a small town about 40 miles from

the nearest city. Everyone in my family couldn't imagine me living in an area that was primarily farmland, since I had lived my entire life in a large city. When my aunt first met my new husband she asked, "What does your father do for a living?" He answered, "He runs a pharmacy." She said, "That's nice. How big a farm does he have?

Ice Rules
by
Carla Jonquil

Having two teenaged daughters, my house was always filled with teens. They felt so much at home there that they regularly would go into the freezer to get ice and make themselves a cold drink. No one ever filled the ice trays. Whenever I would go to fix myself a drink there was never any ice. Only empty ice trays filled my freezer. I constantly was bothered by this. No matter how many times I would tell the kids to fill the ice trays no one ever did. Frustrated, I sat down and wrote out the "Ice Rules". Everyone laughed and thought I had gone over the edge, however, I got my message across clearly! The Ice Rules stayed on our refrigerator door until the girls went to college.

ICE RULES
The 12 Step Program
To be used by anyone and everyone who removes ice from this freezer!
This means YOU!

1. Walk over to the sink with the ice tray in hand.
2. Turn the ice tray over draining remaining water/ice particles from the tray.

3. Turn on the cold water.
4. Hold the ice tray upright under the running water.
5. Wait until the water reaches the top of the tray.
6. Turn the water off.
7. Walk over to the freezer with the ice tray.
8. Open the freezer.
9. Gently add the water filled ice tray into the freezer compartment.
10. Close the freezer door.
11. Wipe off the counter with a dish rag.
12. After several hours open freezer and enjoy ice.

The Computer
by
Eugene Hicks

Our office is low on extra cash for unimportant things like...computers. We all have to share. Just for laughs, I cut out a color picture of a computer from a store advertisement and glued it to a cardboard box. I even made a cardboard keyboard to go with it. I got to work early and set it up on my desk. I waited for my co-workers to see it and get a good laugh. Much to my dismay, no one came into my office that morning.

All of a sudden the picture I had glued to the box slipped off. I picked up the phone and called the secretary. I said, "What's the name of the company that fixes our computers?" "Why" she asked. "Because mine just broke." She said, "But you don't have a computer!" I said, "I most certainly do. Come in and see!" She came running in and we both cracked up. Soon everyone in the office came into my office for a laugh.

Pepper Spray Story
by
Donna Bryne

My brother-in-law had a pepper sprayer
hanging from his belt loop. He was helping a
friend move when the pool table they were
carrying hit against his belt and knocked
against the pepper spray. The can punctured
and pepper spray covered his groin area. We
had to call 911 and take him to the hospital. He
ended up with third degree burns in his groin.
The paramedic that helped him happened to be
at the local bar that afternoon. He retold the
story about the pepper spray rescue. Everyone
in the bar was laughing about the stupidest call
this paramedic had ever been on. "Some idiot",
he said, "actually had a pepper spray can
explode on his crotch." The bartender was my
sister-in-law. "That idiot," she said, "was my
brother!"

Who's That?
by
Marilyn C.

I visit my mother in the nursing home once or
twice a day to be sure she is getting the care she
deserves. She has Alzheimer's Disease. Most of
the time she doesn't even know who I am. One
afternoon we were sitting in her room and she
was looking at a photograph of my brother Jim,
sister Nancy and myself. She pointed to Jim and
said, "This boy looks like my son Jimmy!" I
said, "That is Jim." She said "Oh, and this girl
is so pretty!" she said pointing to my sister
Nancy. I said "Well she is pretty. That's your

daughter Nancy." "Oh." she said and then pointing to my picture she said, "This fat girl over here...I don't know who she is but she don't belong in this picture!" I burst into laughter and then just hugged my mom. "Oh mom, I love you!" She said, "I love you too sweetie. What did you say your name was?"

Black Eyed Peas
- Anonymous

At a crowded noisy craft show, I was displaying my wares while my husband sat and watched. I passed a bit of gas his way. There were so many people talking around our booth that no one heard me. However, my husband took a big inhale of air and as he looked around wide eyed said with a big smile, "MMMMM I smell black eyed peas!" I said "No you don't honey. You smell last nights cabbage!"

Left Foot, Right Foot
by
- Yvonne

When Aubry was little she loved to get dressed by herself. This particular time, she managed to put almost all her snow gear on correctly. I looked at her standing there so proud of herself and said, "You did a great job Aubry except your boots are on the wrong feet." She looked down at her feet and then up at me with terror in her eyes. "But Mom, they're the only feet I've got!"

My Mom is Scary!
- Donnarae Bryne

My Mom and Dad were planning a Halloween party and had rented matching bum costumes. Mom decided to put on her costume and show us girls how funny she looked. While she was upstairs secretly transforming into a bum, Vonnie and I were searching in a hassock where we kept gloves and hats to get ready to go outside and play. With the first sight of the "bum" Vonnie and I were so frightened that we scrambled to get into the hassock to hide. I remember that I was so afraid that I was trembling and that it took mom several minutes to prove to us that she was our mom! She had no idea that we would be so afraid and we had no idea that our pretty "Doris Day mom", a refined and gracious lady could ever look that scary!

Mrs. MaGoo
by
Linda Beckwith

I work as a secretary in a church office. One of my jobs is to type the bulletin for Sunday service. I seem to always make at least one mistake in every bulletin no matter how much I proofread. It is pointed out by my boss every week. One afternoon I walked into her office with a pair of really goofy thick glasses on that I had ordered from a joke catalog. These glasses made my eyes look much bigger than they really were and distorted them a great deal. I said "Like my new glasses? Now I won't make so many mistakes!" We all got a big kick out of that.

PUSH!
by
Yvonne

Aubry was so excited about learning all of her letters. She often read letters off of signs when we were away from home. At a crowded fast food restaurant she stood proudly in front of the trash can and pointed to the letters. She spelled them out loudly, "P-U-S-H" Then she turned and said "Trash!"

Zen Humor - Like a fish out of water
In 1995 as a seasoned adult, I started college. One of my professors suggested I take a philosophy class based on the book Zen and the Art of Motorcycle Maintenance by Robert Pirsig. He said it would broaden my horizons. Well I'm not much for motorcycles and I didn't give two hoots about Zen, but I went anyway. I entered a room of twenty-somethings. They all sported the "unmade bed look" that seems to be so popular with the deep thinking, granola crunching, back pack wearing, save the planet, kiss a whale, hug a tree types. So I sat alone hiding my polished fingernails under the desk and thinking I don't really belong here.

The professor entered and began his lecture with this thought; "We might not really be here." He said mystically, "We might just think we are here!" The class sat at the edge of their seats hanging on his thought. I raised my hand and said, "Hey if you don't see me here next week, don't mark me absent. I'm here, you just don't think I'm here!" And so the sixteen weeks went by with more than a few laughs. I was able to stand it because I was able to laugh. The bonus was that I truly enjoyed that class and learned an enormous amount about myself. I wouldn't have lasted past the first session if I weren't able to laugh a little bit at some of the "Zen like" material we talked about.

The Davis File
A Syracuse Securities Story

While working for a mortgage company one of my co-workers found a funny way to de-stress me one day. I was all upset because I couldn't find a file I needed on a house that was about to close for my clients, Mr. & Mrs. Davis. I ran about the office yelling "Who has the Davis file? - I need the Davis file! - Where is the Davis file?" I really was obnoxious about it and I'm sure getting that upset was not helping me to find the file. Just about the time I was ready to really blow up, my co-worker came in with a nail file he found in a desk drawer. On it he had written The Davis File. He handed it to me and said "Here you go, The Davis File!" It was so stupid that we both got a good laugh out of it and now almost ten years later and I still have The Davis File!

Rear-ended by Some Clown
by
Don Cicchino

Sitting at a stop light minding my own business, I waited for the light to turn green. All of a sudden out of nowhere some clown ran into the back of my car. I jumped out of my car to verbally assault the moron who hit me. When I laid eyes on the assailant it was all I could do to contain myself. There sobbing was a young girl fully dressed in a clown outfit. She had on the red wig and sponge nose, the big goofy collar and all the make up. After calming her down, I drove away with tears of laughter streaming down my face. All I could say over and over was, "I was rear ended by some clown! Really!"

Out To Lunch at the Ball Park
by Gary Simpson

A sweet little old Italian lady walked onto the baseball field with her lawn chair and blanket, opened up her chair and sat down. Settled in and ready to enjoy the game, she was approached by the usher who gently said, "Excuse me miss, but you're not aloud to have a lawn chair." She said innocently, "I no have a my lunch here." He said, "No, no I mean, you can't have your LAWN...CHAIR!" She began to get upset, "I hada my lunch at home! I tolda you, I no havea my lunch here!" Now he was frustrated and searched for a way to help her to understand him. Pointing to the chair he said. "You can't have the CHAIR on the grass!" She hits him in the forehead and said, "Why didn't you say so?" and folded up her chair and walked up to the stands.

The Easter Egg Fiasco

One year my mom decided to make Easter Eggs for each grandchild. She painstakingly drew something personal for each child. The eggs were so beautiful and very special. We all thought Gramma was so sweet to go to such trouble. After the holiday was over my daughter cracked open her egg to find that Gramma had forgotten to cook them. What a mess! But, oh how we laughed!

If you live your life in a joyful way you will be able to find many wonderful stories to hand down to your children. Love one another. Be kind to each other. Learn to forgive. Take a good look at Rover, Spot and Fluffy!

18 Things We Can Learn From A Dog

- Anonymous (Reprinted From Cyberspace)

1. Never pass up the opportunity to go for a joy ride.

2. Allow the experience of fresh air and the wind in your face to be pure ecstasy.

3. When loved ones come home, always run to greet them.

4. When it's in your best interest, practice obedience.

5. Let others know when they've invaded your territory.

6. Take naps, and stretch before rising.

7. Run, romp, and play daily.

8. Eat with gusto and enthusiasm.

9. Be loyal.

10. Never pretend to be something you're not.

11. If what you want is buried, dig until you find it.

12. When someone is having a bad day, be silent, sit close by, and nuzzle.

13. Thrive on attention and let people touch you.

14. Avoid a bite when a simple growl will do.

15. On hot days, drink plenty of water and lie under a shady tree.

16. When your happy, dance around and wag your entire body.

17. Delight in the simple joy of taking a walk.

18. No matter how often you're scolded, don't buy into the guilt thing and pout...run right back and make friends.

YVONNE CONTE

Chapter Ten
Gratitude

"Nothing is quite as funny as the unintended humor of reality." - Steve Allen

The acknowledgment page is typically where the author goes on endlessly thanking people no one has ever heard of for the mundane tasks of typing and editing and yaddah yaddah yaddah! Of course you appreciate these people. What is really interesting to know is; Who are the people who inspired you? Who taught you and encouraged you throughout your life? Who brought you to this page? What did they add to your life that led you to write this book.

Chapter Ten is my way of applauding those people who have continually inspired me with their laughter and encouraged me to laugh along with them. These are the folks who have introduced me to love, taught me the real meaning of success and truly brought joy into my life. My most heartfelt gratitude to all of you.

So, here you are folks. A different kind of acknowledgment page. This is how Yvonne Francine Conte got to this page...

"If it was going to be easy to raise kids, it never would have started with something called labor!"
- Unknown

It was 6:00 in the morning. My younger sister Jacky was savoring her last few minutes of uninterrupted sleep while her husband Mike and four children slept...or so she thought. In stomped her third child, Michele, an adorable four year old. "Mommy", she cried. Jacky turned her head into the pillow as if to erase the intrusion and with her morning voice declared, "Michele, go back to bed it's too early for you to be up." Michele persisted, "But mommy, I got a plane stuck to my head!" Without really listening, Jacky repeated herself, "It's too early Michele! Go back to..." Then hearing the hum of a small motor, she opened one eye to find a green toy plane stuck to Michele's head. "What in the world??" Apparently, her son Peter wound up the plane's wheels and then struck Michele on the head with it. The wheels began to spin and got entirely entangled in her long hair ripping at its roots. This story is not funny. What is funny, is that Jacky made the poor child pose for a picture, before she rescued her hair from the attack of the green plane! Now that is funny!

Caution Laughter is Contagious

John Gabriel made milk come out of my nose at the Friendly's restaurant in Ithaca, New York. John and I sold telephone systems for a national interconnect. It was not an uncommon scene to find us laughing together, however, this was by far the all time laugh festival!

We started out down the highway like we always did, looking for businesses where we might make a "cold call". First we got sidetracked when we stopped for coffee and John noticed that he could see right through my skirt. We stopped at a nearby mall to buy a slip. They were having a sidewalk sale and we found it unthinkable not to shop just a little bit! I bought a "Clock A Book", a black patent leather purse with a built in clock the size of your average school clock, for just $3.97. I never used the Clock A Book as a purse. However, I took it out and showed it to anyone who came by just because we thought it was the most outrageous thing we ever saw. I later put it in a garage sale and it was the topic of conversation all afternoon. I sold it to a man who said, "My wife will crack up over this one!" My $3.97 investment brought miles of smiles to a host of fellow laughers. Now back to that day on the road with my good friend John.

After several "cold calls" we decided to stop at Friendly's restaurant for lunch. For no apparent reason we started to make a list of names, that, when said fast, sounded like something else. We started off with the easy ones like, Patty O'Furniture, Ginger Snap and Ben Dover. Once we got started we just couldn't stop. In the beginning several people began to look at us strangely because we were laughing so much. We laughed so hard at some of our concoctions that soon all the people in the restaurant were laughing at us laughing. The manager came over to fill our coffee cups and said, "I don't know what is so funny but you are welcome to come back and entertain us again, anytime."

We did not sell a single telephone system that day. However, we were able to think up 308 names that made us laugh till the milk came out our noses.

The Little Town With The Big Heart

Thank you Edmeston, New York for opening your hearts and homes to a lost young girl some twenty eight years ago. So many people in this tiny village, hidden somewhere between Cooperstown and Utica, are responsible for making a positive difference in my life. In Edmeston I learned what a church family is and what the words neighbor and friendship really mean. Thank you Marie and Gil Dravland for introducing me to the Methodist faith and teaching me how to become a part of it. Thank you Betty Ann Chesebrough and Dani Nonenmacher for introducing me to lifelong friendships.

Edmeston Central School is where I experienced teachers who took a genuine interest in their students. Mr. Charlie Rider, Mr. Bob Nonenmacher, Mrs. Doris Holdredge, Mr. Howie

Lull, Mrs. Audrey Lohnas, Mrs. Janet Bowen, Mr. Larry Gay, Mrs. Gerry Saunders: thank you for taking an interest. My dear Edmestonians, you will always be very special to me.

If anyone is looking for a great place to raise a family, take route eight south to Leonardsville and take a left up over the hill to Edmeston. You'll love it!

Southern Born Brother-In-Law

Eugene moved into our family from Shreveport, Louisiana and has not stopped making me laugh for almost twenty years. Gene tried every way to conform to our grand Italian family. He went to work for my father and did exactly as he was told.

One afternoon Dad told Gene to get a folding chair and follow him. Like a puppy after his new master, Gene quickly picked up a chair and ran down the long hallway after him. Dad walked towards the bathroom and Gene followed with the chair in hand. Then Dad walked into the bathroom, turned and looked at Gene and the chair. Bewildered, Gene handed Dad the chair and stood outside in the hall and waited patiently. Dad began to laugh behind the door and eventually Gene asked the question Dad had been waiting for. "Dad", he paused as if to carefully choose his words, "What are you doing with the chair in the bathroom?" Dad said, "You don't want me to get 'it' wet do you?" He opened the door and the two began to laugh out loud. "I've been pulling this prank on my new employee's for the past twenty years", Dad said between howls of laughter, "No one has ever made it all the way to the bathroom with the chair until you!"

Gene quickly became the fix-it man around the office. One evening Dad was working at his desk with a nice young couple who were ready to sign on the dotted line. Gene was in the ceiling above them trying to repair some faulty wiring. He accidentally stepped on an unsupported ceiling tile and fell through the ceiling! Landing on all fours, smack in the middle of Dads big oak desk, he simply said, "Oopps!" Dad looked at him and casually said, "You planning on being here long?" Gene unceremoniously said, "Actually, I'm almost done." and walked out of the office carrying several pieces of broken ceiling tile with him as Dad finished the sale! Thanks for the many years of laughter brother-in-law.

The Unparalleled Gift of Joy

On February 1, 1973 I curled the delicate hand of a precious little girl around my finger and experienced true joy. Everyone who meets her sees a very gifted, insightful, energetic, no nonsense, take charge kind of gal. I know the tender, compassionate side of her. If you are fortunate enough to be her friend, you have a friend eternally. If you need anything, she will find a way to produce it for you. If something has to get done, she will stay with it until it is completed. I am very proud of her. Nothing I have experienced compares to how I feel. I thank my daughter, Aubry Lynn Ludington for teaching me the meaning of true joy.

My Very Own Mr. Saturday Night

The idea for this book may never have existed without the incredible humor of my son, John Ludington. One rainy morning in 1989 I sat at my kitchen table in tears. After fifteen years in sales, I was completely burned out and really did not know what I was going to do next. John looked at me with his warm genuine smile and simply said, "Why don't you be a comedian, Mom?" That was just the beginning. The seed he planted that morning grew into this wonderful profession full of meaning for me.

I thank John for the endless hours of side splitting laughter around the kitchen table and in the car on the way to school. His wacky faces, numerous accents and dialects, imitations and inventive characters have both entertained and delighted me for all of his twenty-three years. Many times when I felt like I just could not walk another step, his silliness carried me. I could never have made it without him! I pray he grows old, but never grows up - he is my rock!

I feel compelled to put this in writing for all the world to see. Aubry and John have continually been very motivating, encouraging forces in my life. I stand strong today because they have always stood beside me with love and support.

Stupid is as Stupid Does

Thank you to the traffic cop in Utica, New York who, when asked for directions, actually did say to me, "You can't get there from here." (He was dead serious!) To all the strangers that I have ever watched accidentally trip and then act as if they did not, I thank you for the chuckle.

———————————

Education does not answer questions;
it provokes them.

Especially, I wish to acknowledge the professors at Monroe Community College in Rochester, New York. Their constant encouragement, inspiration and enthusiastic support and belief in me was instrumental beyond belief. Thank you Nancy Mallory, Tom Proietti, Barry Goldfarb, Dave Smith and Bob Herzog for the many hours of laughter and learning.

———————————

It All Begins at Home

A heartfelt thank you to all my funny family members. Especially my three sisters, who make Curley, Larry and Moe look like accountants! Annie can impersonate all the characters from the Wizard of Oz and is also a gifted air guitarist. Jacky continues to produce laughter each day with her unpredictable children and my hero Donnarae - she just makes every day a birthday party!

Most of all I thank my father and mother, Frank and Angela Conte. Their wonderful fresh sense of humor filled our home with laughter and our hearts with joy and left us with priceless memories. I believe we all begin as incredible, creative, curious and unafraid children. Some of us stay that way thanks to a childhood full of non- judgmental fun. I treasure all my moments of fun!

As Bullwinkle and Rocky used to say, -And now for something completely different...", I offer you a challenge. Add more laughter and humor and just plain fun to your life. Give the gift of laughter to your children, to your spouse and to your co-workers.

Take advantage of every opportunity open to you. Use the ideas noted in this book and create some of your own. Find ways to add humor and laughter to your life and the lives of people you love. I hope you have not just acquired information from **Serious Laughter**, but that you have formed some new and healthy habits!

Most important, whatever you do have fun doing it!! Thank you for taking the time to read **Serious Laughter**. I wish for you only the best of times.

Be happy my friends.
Live your life so that your epitaph reads,
"Not one single regret."

- Yvonne

References

Cousins, Norman. <u>Anatomy of an Illness</u>. New York: W.W.Norton & Co., 1979.

Bauman, M. Garrett. <u>Idea and Details</u>. Harcourt Brace & Company., 1995

Sunshine, Linda.
<u>The Illustrated WOODY Allen Reader</u> New York Alfred A. Knopf, Inc., 1993

Carnegie, Dale.
<u>How to Stop Worrying and Start Living</u>. New York Simon & Schuster., 1984

King James Version. <u>Holy Bible</u>
Zondervan Bible Publishers

Meyer, Michele. "Laughter It's Good Medicine"
<u>Better Homes and Gardens</u>, April 1997: 72-.76

Nachman, Barbara. "RX: A dose of chuckles"
<u>Gannett News Service Democrat and Chronicle</u>
April 7th, 1997

Lansky, Vicki. "52 Ways to Change Your Life"
<u>Ladies Home Journal</u> January 1996: 154

"Your Partner's Health" <u>McCall's</u> August 1995

Keiffer, Elisabeth. "How to Boost Your Immune System" <u>Woman's Day</u> October 1995: 96 & 98

McIntosh, Claire. "7 Habits of Close Couples"
<u>McCall's</u> January 1998

Looking for a good book?
These are the books I Love

<u>You will be able to accomplish anything you want and improve your communication skill greatly if you read:</u>

Creative Visualization - Shakti Gawain
Positive Imaging - Norman Vincent Peale
See you At The Top - Zig Ziglar
Power Thoughts - Robert Schuller
What to Say When You Talk To Yourself
    - Shad Helmstetter, Ph.D.
How to Stop Worrying and Start Living
    - Dale Carnegie
Enrich Your Life - Dale Carnegie
How to Enjoy Your life and your Job
    - Dale Carnegie
Do It! Let's get off our Butts
    - John Roger & Peter McWilliams
The Road Less Traveled - M. Scott Peck, MD
Wishcraft - Barbara Sher & Annie Gottlieb
University of Success - OG Mandino
Human Options - Norman Cousins
How to Win Customers and Keep Them for Life
    - Michael LeBocuf

<u>You will know a lot more about yourself if you read:</u>

Do What You Love and The Money Will Follow
    - Marsha Sinetar
Leaving The Enchanted Forest
    - Stephanie Covington and Liana Beckett
Make The Connection - Oprah Winfrey
Simple Abundance - A Daybook of Comfort and Joy
    - Sarah Van Breathnach

<u>You will understand a lot more about comedy if
you read:</u>

Getting Even - Woody Allen
Without Feathers - Woody Allen
Side Effects - Woody Allen
The Woody Allen Companion - Stephen Spingnesi
Sunday Nights at Seven - Jack Benny
Enter Talking - Joan Rivers
Still Talking - Joan Rivers
Wake Me When It's Funny - Garry Marshall
One More Time - Carol Burnett
Leading With My Chin - Jay Leno
Pretend The World Is Funny - Rhoda Fisher

<u>You better have a box of kleenex if you read:</u>

It's Always Something - Gilda Radner
The Bridges of Madison County - James Waller

ORDER FORM

Please use this order form for additional copies of

Serious Laughter

Please send me:

Quantity: _____ Serious Laughter @ $16.95 each.

Shipping & Handling:
$2.50 for first book, $1.50 for each additional book.

Sales Tax:
New York State residents please add sales tax.

Total Amount Enclosed: $_____

Name_____

Address_____

City_____State_____Zip____

Payment: Please make check or money order
for full amount payable to:

Crack-A-Smile
send to:
Crack-A-Smile
262 Culver Road
Rochester, NY 14607-2332

For further information or comments:
Phone: (716) 256-2916   Fax: (716) 256-7441

Quantity discounts are also available
I would like to receive information about the
Humor Workshop and other Crack-A-Smile
programs _____

Please use this form to order:
Humor First Aid Kits, Clown noses and Smile on a Sticks

Please send me:

Total

△ Red Sponge Clown Nose @ $1.50 each

_____

△ Humor First Aid Kits @ $15.00 each   _____

△ Smile on A Stick @ $2.50 each   _____

Shipping & Handling:
Under $30.00   add $2.50   _____
$30.00 - $50.00   add $5.00
NY State residents please add sales tax. _____

Total Amount Enclosed: $ _____
Please allow 7-14 business days for delivery.

Name_____

Address_____

City_____State_____Zip____

Payment:
Please make check or money order for full amount
payable to
Crack-A-Smile
send to:

Crack-A-Smile
262 Culver Road
Rochester, NY 14607-2332

For further information or comments:
Phone: (716) 256-2916   Fax: (716) 256-7441
E-mail: von@frontiernet.net